ALL the ADAMS in the WORLD

UNDERSTANDING the AWE and AWFUL in AUTISM
A Thirty-Year Journey

SHEILA SILVER

PAGE PUBLISHING, INC.
Conneaut Lake, PA

First originally published by Page Publishing 2020

ISBN 978-1-68456-439-2 (pbk)
ISBN 978-1-68456-441-5 (hc)
ISBN 978-1-68456-440-8 (digital)

Printed in the United States of America

To the friends, family, teachers, care givers and good people who
have held my hand through this journey—Adam and I thank you.

I, Wynne Silver

Every story begins before the story begins, and not surprisingly, so does mine. I didn't have any idea of this until Adam was six years old. That was in 1993. But the story begins twenty years earlier in 1973 when I was only seventeen. Long before I knew there would be a son named Adam.

...I could hug my dad one more time.

My father had his first heart attack in January 1969. Here was this vital, charismatic leader of a man who was struck down while sitting in a colleague's office. He never got over the shame of having lost his sloppy joes over another man's desk. All a heart patient could do to recover in those days was "rest"—a word not part of my Marine Corps sergeant father's personality. Oh sure, he had been out of the Marines since 1945, but one would not know this through observation of the way he ran his life, his family, his home, his school, the world. "When Silver drives, everybody drives!" he would yell out the window of the 1964 Rambler. Not certain what this meant—we just knew that whenever dad would tell us to jump—we damn well better ask, "How far?"

We thought that living under the auspices of "Don't upset your father—you could kill him" was tough enough on three teenage kids—until things got even worse. He was only forty-six years old and had already been living with his "heart condition" for four years, but in 1973, another bigger, harder, more damaging heart attack hit. And later that night as he lay in the ICU hooked up to all sorts of machines, the stroke came. As I stood at his bedside holding his hand, he looked at me through pleading eyes; I thought his inability to speak was because he was so drugged up. A few, long hours later, we would hear the words *stroke*, *paralysis*, and *aphasia*. Our lives were forever changed. Our father was never again able to tell us how far to jump.

Dad was only 5'6", but to me he was a giant.

A giant personality.

A giant commander.

The king of his own castle.

He held a master's in communications, was a charismatic public speaker, and held court in our living room as he ranted about politics, public education, and his numerous pet peeves, one of whom was me.

The stroke took away our father's speech.

He was completely paralyzed, from top to bottom, on his right side.

He would never return to the work he loved—middle school principal.

Today doctors would say that our dad had "locked-in syndrome"—but in 1973 there was no such euphemism. The stroke has struck him down. "Like flies to wanton boys are we to the gods," says Gloucester in Shakespeare's *King Lear*, "they use us for their sport."

It was his larger-than-life Marine Corps sergeant personality that kept him going for five more years; his determination never faltering.

He learned to walk.

He learned to drive.

He learned to eat and write with his left hand.

He practiced speaking over a CB radio that sat on our kitchen table. His handle was Mr. Principal. It was a slow, indiscernible speech—first vowels, then consonants, then a few words. And face-less supporters would encourage him to keep on trying—"Copy that, Mr. Principal." We learned to read his face, his eyes, his sounds. With grunts, he would express his disdain for politics, public education, and his numerous pet peeves. And he found two words "Oh boy!" to express both delight and disgust.

For five years I traveled with him twice a week to speech, occu-pational and physical therapy. I would watch, listen and then be taught the exercises to do with him at home. We would also go out on weekly excursions to the barber shop, the tailor, the local mall, the movies, even to his favorite restaurant, Sizzler. It was on these public outings where I was first introduced to "The Look" given to us by others. I learned to read expressions of curiosity, judgment, and pity. The condescending childlike tones used to greet him were common, as most people just assumed that because he could not speak, he could not understand. I would see tears well up in the hearts and eyes of those who remembered him from "*before*," but as the years went by, fewer and fewer came around. Time moved on and so did people. Well-meaning strangers would whisper platitudes into my ear, "You're such a good daughter," but I could feel only shame and guilt because of my hidden resentment for having to stay home to help care for him instead of going away to college.

I believe that our father would measure his greatest achievement during those five years of recovery to have been on the day of my sister's wedding. On April 9, 1978, our father walked my sister down the aisle to the tears of all assembled. My sister holding the paralyzed right arm, Dad grasping onto the three-legged steel cane with his left, we all held our breath in anticipation of the moment he had to speak. He had rehearsed these four words for weeks, but none of us was sure, himself most of all, if the words would come out.

"Who gives this woman away?"

Wait for it—wait for it—then slowly and oh so deliberately, "Her mother and I."

The congregation roared with applause.

The remarkable thing about our dad is that he woke up every morning singing. To the end, he really loved life. Two months after my sister's wedding he was hit by his last and most devastating stroke, and he succumbed into a coma. There he stayed for five months— from the day of that last stroke—to the day his insurance ran out.

He was that determined to control life until the end.

I loved our father as much as I feared him. Not a day has gone by over the past forty years that I still do not subconsciously seek his approval. He is the most courageous man I have ever known, and as relieved as I felt when he breathed his last breath, I still wish that I had been given even one more day to take him to the therapies and support him in his recovery.

Wishes do come true.

CHAPTER 2

Terror in the Night

Our first son, Joshua, was only a year old when we became pregnant with number 2. He was a planned baby, and we were thrilled. Our dream was to have four children—me—because I was the middle of three, and kitchen tables were never made for a family of five. I was always stuck on the end—not really a part of the table. And his father was tied for last—"one of the twins," by which, even in his sixties, he is still referred. Tied for last—he resented this label his entire life. So our decision was that between 3 and 5 was the number 4, a table for a family of six. That was our plan, and we were sticking to it.

I was so beyond in *love* with our firstborn. I *loved* being a mother. It was the role I was born to play. I was so happy and fulfilled being a mom, reveling in every step of our son's growth. Joshua Wynne was a baby of pure joy—he lit up the hearts of all. And he enjoyed everything—truly *everything*—and so did we. This first year of our number 1's life was a treasure—we were solid as a couple, as parents, and we anticipated the birth of our second child with excitement. However, I had lots of worries before the birth of number 2. Not about the delivery or his health. Oh! And I just knew that we were having a brother for Josh!

My fear was in questioning my capacity to love number 2. When I became a mom, I found a depth of love in me that I never knew existed. My fear was that I might not be able to love a second child as much as I loved my first. How could I ever love another baby with the passion and joy that I gave so fully to Josh? And would I have to hold back from loving number 1 to spread the love to our number 2?

We had such a good life. We owned a lovely little home, just big enough for three, lived in a safe family community. Both teachers, we made good salaries that allowed us to provide for our little family, travel, enjoy theater, and most importantly, we had our summer, winter and spring vacations together. Close to my school, I would drop the baby off at daycare at 8:30 a.m. and pick him up by 3:00 p.m. It was a fine balance, and we were happy. I just did not know how we would divide our time and our love with the arrival of number 2. *What were we thinking?*

Adam was a planned C-section, unlike Josh, who after twenty hours of hard labor—and I do mean *hard labor*—had to be taken out in an emergency. This time, I looked great for the delivery pictures; all I had to do was lie on the table and receive the local anesthetic for the surgery. The moment that precious baby was put in my arms, all my fears melted away. Another door in my heart fully opened, and the love came flowing out for our second baby boy—Adam Louis. As I held him and felt his sweet, warm body next to mine, I laughed at myself for having doubted my capacity to love.

There were things that I did not know until after the delivery. Concerns that my doctor had prepared for that had been kept from me. My amniotic fluid had dried up. The baby's heartbeat had accelerated so high that an infant specialist had been brought up on emergency call "just in case." I lollygagged in the euphoria of demerol and did not tune into the hushed conversations among the delivery team. His dad had been right there with me, holding my hand and keeping me distracted. I knew nothing of these advanced preparations for which the team had prepped, because after he was delivered, cleaned up, and put into my arms, he was pronounced "perfect." So perfect in fact, that my doctor took an early departure so that she could get to the grand opening of the Mervyn's Department store in our city—an event that would be commemorated every July 18 along with Adam's birthday.

I did not see Josh until the next morning and the twenty-month-old baby, whom I had kissed goodbye on Saturday morning before going to the hospital, had become a little boy overnight. He was so excited to meet his brother and to give Mommy a hug and a kiss. My heart burst with joy. We were now a family of four—and I was so happy. Maybe a table for four would be a better plan.

Adam had a typical development or as his doctor would generally write, "Unremarkable." Having already experienced the numerous first milestones with Josh, we knew Adam was "right on schedule" as we had the thrill of watching him hold up his head and then sit up on his own, begin the bug butt scrunch, rocking, and then begin to crawl, with smiles and coos. He wasn't particularly fussy, and he would especially light up when Josh came into play. Josh was a great "big brother," and we adjusted to being a family of four with relative ease.

I could take an entire semester off school to be with our now two-year-old and newborn sons, but in February 1988, I returned to work. Both boys went together to day care at Aunt Judy's Playhouse. Judy would write in a journal each day sharing what the boys had done, and we counted the days to the president's weekend, spring break, and of course, summer! We reasoned that having our vacation time off together that teaching allowed was worth the tradeoff of having our sons in day care. Dropped off at 8:30 a.m. and picked up by 3:00 p.m., they slept, they ate, and they played in a daily routine that had them well rested and excited when I would arrive to pick them up. Sure, it was hectic getting out of the house each morning, but except for the endless piles of essays that loomed over my head, our family time was ours. Dinner, more playtime, bath time, reading, and then bed. The boys were asleep by eight, and I would get out the red pen while their dad spent his night hours watching television. Teaching second grade did not demand the level of planning and grading as teaching high school English. By the time their dad came upstairs to bed, it would be time for me to get up for Adam's late-night feeding. Yes, I was tired, and it was not uncommon for me fall asleep sitting on the couch while feeding Adam, waking up in the stillness of the early hours of the morning with a crimped neck and peaceful baby in my arms. It was our routine, part of the responsibilities that come with parenting, and we accepted that we were tired—but look what we had created! We loved looking at the boys when they were asleep. What parent doesn't? We felt blessed and began to think ahead. We decided to wait two years before trying for number 3, at which time Josh would be five years old and Adam would be three. Silly me, believing that our plan would move forward as scheduled.

What surprised me as a new mom, one who had never spent time with babies when I was growing up, was how their personalities and preferences were so clear from the moment they entered the world outside me. Josh was lively, funny, and performing, singing and dancing from an early age. Adam was introspective, an observer of his brother's antics, and although he loved being sung to and entertained by his older brother, when given the option, he would always choose his books. He loved books—the pictures, the shapes, the textures. I could endlessly read *Good Night, Moon* or *Pat the Bunny* while he cuddled in my lap. He especially loved the books on baby animals, and he would point at the pictures and make their baby animal sounds. In describing my sons, I would say, "Josh will be my performer and Adam my poet."

And at each checkup, our pediatrician would report on Adam's development, typically "normal" according to the milestone indicators on infant development charts. Most of our friends were young couples with young children, and except for the fact the he was mine and most unique, wonderful, and special, I cannot say that Adam's first year of life was not progressing as T. Berry Brazelton told us it should. Adam loved to be loved, to be hugged, to reach out to Mommy, Daddy, and Josh. By July 1988, he had begun to explore the immediate world outside the playpen. Life was great, and we were content. Or so we pretended.

The night terrors began when Adam was eight months old. In the wee hours of the morning, he would begin to scream in what sounded like agonizing pain. Red faced, gasping for breath, he would wail and arch his little body. There were no tears, only writhing shrieks of agony. Nothing could comfort him. His heartbeat and pulse would jump out of his skin as he became visibly overheated. He would not let us pick him up or hold him. If we tried, he would howl more loudly, like a wounded animal in fear for its life. Our pediatrician told us not to worry, that this is not unusual and that it would pass. "Just make sure you get some rest too, Mom and Dad," Dr. Huckaby would say in his gentle, pediatric, Southern drawl. We trusted him and did our best not to worry.

We researched everything we could find on this not-so-written-about subject, but all sources concurred with Dr. Huckaby: we should not worry: "Children usually don't remember anything about their sleep terrors in the morning" (www.mayoclinic.org/diseases-conditions/night-terrors/basics/symptoms/com).

We became stealth parents, silently hovering over Adam as he slept, trying to figure out what was going on that would jolt him into this nightly anguished state. We feared that in his flailing, he would hurt himself, as much as a nine-, ten-, eleven-month-old could hurt himself. The more we tried to touch him, caress him, comfort him, the more he would appear to fear us. His eyes were wide open, wild with intensity, but we could not reach him. He was not awake, and he was inconsolable.

Our neighbors began to complain about the noise. We were sure we would be investigated for child abuse. One of us would pick up Adam's tense and rigid body nearly smothering him close to our chests as we carried him out of the house, while the other scurried ahead to open the doors. We figured that the best we could do was to get him into the car, strap him safely in his car seat, and then drive around Irvine until he fell back to sleep. We took turns being the chauffeur. Often, the night's driver would stay with Adam in the car when we returned home so as not to risk waking him up. When the 5:30 a.m. alarm would ring, we would alternate sitting in the car or getting ourselves and Josh ready for the day. We began to put Adam to sleep in the clothes he would wear the next day. We simply wanted to reduce the stress he was experiencing in any way possible. We had to find ways to make this work for all four of us.

And like the experts told us, when he woke up in the morning, Adam was his sweet, gentle self, seeking Mommy or Daddy to hold him and wanting us to read his favorite book. Only his puffy face and red, swollen eyes told the real story. That and the black eye I had once or twice from when he conked me in full thrust in the face with the back of his head as I carried him to the car.

In July, we celebrated his first birthday to the enjoyment of all. Adam loved his clown cake and his favorite present was his first Dr. Seuss book. We read *Go Dog Go* so many times that before we ever heard *Mommy* or *Daddy*, his first word was *Seuss*. His days were filled with curiosity and beginning language, he discovered new foods along with learning how to walk. By day he was right on schedule. By night his dad and I prepared for the hours ahead, anxiously awaiting the screams when we would jump into action. If a night or two went by without a terror incident, we would become hopeful that he had outgrown them, only to be heartbroken when we would find ourselves once again driving around Irvine at two in the morning.

In November, Joshua turned three and began a real preschool at *Ms. Linda's*. He was so happy to be in a "big boy" school. It was the first time our sons would be apart during the day, and worry as we did, we did not notice any impact upon Adam. He stayed with Ms. Judy having a good old time! The pattern of good days and night terrors continued. We did the best we could do and hoped that sooner or later they would subside, God willing, sooner than later. But that was not to be.

On January 28, 1989, eighteen months and ten days after the day he was born, the switch turned off. The life went out of Adam's eyes. He shut down. He stopped interacting with us, and we did not hear him speak again until he was seven years old. He lost expression in his face, showed interest in nothing, and in most ways, returned to being a helpless infant. Only his physical abilities remained intact.

We were bereft.

We were about to embark on a year of diagnostic testing, fear, frustration, and distress.

What cruel magician's illusionary trick made our son disappear?

CHAPTER 3

Missing Adam

"Relax. Would you stop it? There's nothing wrong." But there was something wrong, something really wrong, and I could not get Adam's dad to accept this. Adam had stopped talking. Adam had stopped looking at us. He did not smile, interact, or engage. Adam still had night terrors. Where had my baby gone?

"Stop looking for things that aren't there." He was right; so many things that used to be there were no longer there. But you cannot force a person to see something if he refuses to see it. It's not that Adam's dad didn't notice the changes; he just did not want to see them. He could not acknowledge that we were no longer a "perfect family"—not that we ever were. And larger than that, if there was ever any hint of acknowledgment that something was wrong, we were not allowed to take it outside our home. And so began my solo journey as a mom and my efforts to solve the puzzle of the missing Adam. Denial—it's a powerful thing. Call it mother's intuition, or call it what it was, but I would not stop until I figured out what was wrong with Adam.

After repeated visits to the pediatrician where I clamored for support, Dr. Huckaby calmly shared that there was evidence of developmental delays, and so began the quest for answers. If there is one thing that I am good at, it is springing into action. And so, I did.

Before chronicling the next year, I need to tell you that everything, *everything*, takes time—a lot of time. From recommendation to referral to scheduling to having the appointment, everything takes a long, long time. We were about to contribute a new chapter to Joseph Heller's *Catch 22*—'Major Major.'

Adam was too young to be given a diagnosis, and without a diagnosis, it is very difficult to get services. Thus, began diagnostic testing. Although insurance did not cover diagnostic testing, there was no price too costly when it came to helping our son.

March 1989

Because the first noticeable change was in Adam's failure to respond to our voices, our search began with the possibility that he had lost his hearing. We were referred to Buena Park Speech and Language Center where headsets were placed over Adam's ears through which he would listen to sounds and then given tasks to complete—point to the red ball, what animal makes this sound, raise your hand when you hear the bell. Nothing. Not sure if he heard a thing. For the first twenty minutes, he screamed and kept pulling off the headsets. "Mom, can you please make him keep these on?" requested the intern. The tests were never completed and all we accomplished was traumatizing Adam with the headsets.

April 1989

Our pediatrician also thought it would be valuable for Adam to see an infant psychiatrist to assess if our son had experienced any emotional trauma. Now I am a very therapeutic person; I knew how messed up I was and had been in therapy off and on since 1980, when I first began to work on the effects of my Marine Corps father's (circa 1950) *theories* of child raising (we were no Cleaver family) and then, the impact of his heart attacks and strokes. Remember how I shared how worried I was that I would not be able to love my second baby as much as I loved the first? Therapy. And my husband's denial of Adam's regression? I knew better than to deal with that all alone. Therapy. So the suggestion that we take Adam to be seen by the head of infant psychiatry at University California Irvine—UCI was a perfectly reasonable referral—at $700 per hour, for a minimum of three hours. Twice a week for three weeks, we met with Dr. C and after the check for $4,800 cleared, we received the report that the only thing wrong with Adam was that he was suffering from separation anxiety because I was a working mother. Dr. C's recommendation was that I needed to quit my job and personally see him for a minimum of six months. Then, when I got myself together, Adam would start talking again. Adam's dad reveled in this diagnosis, "I told you so," and did not spare any glee in blaming Adam's condition on me, to which I replied "*Bullshit!*" in anguish. As I have shared, I am a very therapeutic person, and if there in one thing I know about myself, it is that I am *not* a "refrigerator mom," labeled by Bruno Bettelheim in the 1960s. I am a drama teacher, for God's sake; I wear my emotions on my sleeve; love reeks out of my every pore; I cry at Hallmark commercials. To say I was infuriated was an understatement. This was abuse, a punch against the working mother, a male Freudian slander against women. It catapulted me into further action to learn what was wrong and to help my son. But the damage had been done. Not just within me, which was plenty, but in the great divide of my marriage.

May 1989

The morning was set for our appointment at Children's Hospital of Orange County (CHOC) where Adam would be given an ABR (auditory brainstem response) test designed to measure the brain's electric auditory responses to sound and detect hearing loss type, degree, and if there is any auditory nerve and brainstem damage. It was here that the words "brain tumors" were first introduced. It was all so frightening. As Adam sat on my lap, the team approached him with bundles of wires and electrodes to be attached to his head. If you consider the way he reacted to a pair of headphones, just try to imagine what happened when it looked like an octopus was going to be attached to his head. "Mom, can you please get him to calm down." The decision was made for him to be sedated and to administer the test when he was asleep. He spat out the liquid sedative, and plan B was to give him a shot. It took three of us to hold him down. When groggy enough not to notice, the electrodes were placed on his scalp, and the nurses came to take him from my arms. "No, that is not going to happen." I climbed onto the gurney, and together we were wheeled into the testing room. Dark and cold, I lay next to Adam as a series of lights, sounds and pulses went off and on—on and off—he felt nothing. The tests revealed that his brain and hearing were responding perfectly well and so, he was not deaf. Really? Then *why* was he not responding?

Not believing their results, I started conducting my own tests. I would stand directly behind Adam while he was eating, and I would yell his name. He did not turn around. He did not blink. But then while he was looking at books in his room, I would put on his favorite Disney sing-along video at the lowest possible volume, and he would come running out of his room, down the hallway into the family room, happy to be able to watch "Zippidy-Doo-Dah." It was baffling. He can hear; he can definitely hear.

June 1989

"Have you heard of Regional Center, Mom?" inquired Dr. Huckaby. "I think our next step is to have Adam tested there." Now, here is where things began to get really complicated. Regional Centers are nonprofit private corporations that contract with the Department of Developmental Services to provide or coordinate services and supports for individuals with developmental disabilities. The great news is that we live in California and have close access to these services.

The bad news is that to have access to Regional Center, you must have a referral from a behavioral specialist who states that he/she is not able to meet the needs of a client, hence necessitating the need for services from Regional Center. So we first had to have Adam tested by a behaviorist who would give Adam an initial diagnosis and who would also be willing to *not* treat our son for his developmental delays. No practitioner wants to label a child under the age of three, so I had no idea where to turn. In the meantime, the tension in our home increased as Adam's dad would insist that it was my fault because I refused to see Dr. C for therapy—"*The problem isn't with Adam.*" He would back off when I would ask how we would pay for my therapy, especially when I had to quit my job? I was continuing to hear, "Relax, there's nothing wrong. After all, even if Adam is diagnosed with something, there is nothing we can do until he is three years old. You *need* to stop this. You are driving us crazy and hurting Adam. *You* need to go see Dr. C."

What was I supposed to do? Should I really submit myself to working with an abusive, misogynistic psychiatrist and ignore what I knew to be true—that every day that went by without knowing was another day in delaying getting help for Adam? *No.* I was unwilling to wait another fourteen months until Adam turned three. *That's a lot of time.* I took myself back to my therapist. The issues were far deeper than my son.

It was here that I began a new way of thinking that would prove to be of value for the next twenty-nine years—that would be until today—February 1, 2019, because I still practice this belief daily. And I will continue to proceed with this belief tomorrow and tomorrow and tomorrow, of that I am sure. I hold an inherent belief that with so many people in the world, even before the days of the internet and social media, that somebody will know somebody who will know somebody, who, regardless of the degrees of separation, will be willing to help us. And so it was. I knew someone who had just completed her MA in speech therapy at California State Northridge, who knew a professor who was the advisor to another grad student who was finishing her MA in developmental diagnostic testing, who had just received her initial placement at Children's Hospital of Los Angeles, who was conducting a study on the reliability of diagnostic testing in children under the age of three. Through my friend, who knew the professor, who knew the grad student who was conducting her research at CHoLA, Adam become part of the study. Four visits later, after twisting and turning, matching colors, identifying puzzle pieces by shape and stacking blocks, Adam was given the diagnosis of PDD (pervasive developmental delay). It was enough of a diagnosis to get us into the doors of a Regional Center; PDD had not been recognized as an official diagnosis in the soon-to-be-published *DSM III* (*Diagnostic and Statistical Manual of Mental Disorders*, Third Edition, by the American Psychiatric Institute), so our insurance would not cover additional testing, but at what price? We did not have to wait until Adam was three.

July 1989

We spent Adam's second birthday at the Regional Center, where he was given the Bailey diagnostic test for the fifth time. He had memorized the steps and what to do. Of course, he did. The question becomes, *why* the urgency to hook up with Regional Center? What I want to point out here is that I had no map for this journey. I was walking blindly through each step, hoping above hope that the next person I met, whomever that person might be, might point me in the next direction. I was living in a labyrinth, a maze of unknowns through which I anxiously traveled. Remember, it was only 1989, and long before the word *autism* ever entered my mind, the only thing we knew about autism was that Dustin Hoffman had won an academy award for *Rainman*. So *why* the urgency to hook up with Regional Center? In my limited understanding, Regional Center was the funding source for any services that might be recommended for Adam. *But*—and this is a *huge* but—the caveat was that a child has to be developmentally deficit in a minimum of three areas to receive funding and services. And now a plethora of new possibilities entered the picture. And I found myself wondering, what was I rooting for? Did I want Adam to be communicatively, socially, physically, receptively, expressively, or cognitively delayed? And in how many areas? And would he reach the magic number of 75 percent so that he could receive services, or would it be better to max out at, say, 73 percent so that I could sigh a huge breath of relief that my son was not so impaired to have to become a client of Regional Center? Truthfully, from the top of my head to the deepest core of my soul, I knew that something was very, very wrong with my son. Do I hope that he is severe enough to need help or falls short just enough to not be given a label? And all this while what I really want to be doing is eating cake and singing "Happy Birthday".

The first time he was tested at Regional Center, I was asked not to be in the room, so he cried the entire time and could not be tested. The results were recorded as inconclusive. The second time he was tested at Regional Center, I was allowed to be in the room with him, but so were the twenty-two new trainees observing how to administer the Bailey diagnostic. The results were recorded as inconclusive. Adam was given one more opportunity for testing, and during the third time, he stacked the blocks and matched the shapes and colors, but he did not make eye contact, nor did he speak or respond to questions. That was also the day that the letters "FHE" first showed up when given a crayon and some paper. The results were recorded as "Cognitively impaired. Receptive language—six months. Expressive language—two months." Congratulations, Adam. You made the required 75 percent developmental deficit. Success? Now we could move onto obtaining services.

I spent the rest of the afternoon in and out of the bathroom throwing up these results.

"Please, please, God, give me patience."

God gave me exactly what I prayed for.

God gave me autism.

My wish had been granted—I had been given more days than I can count to take my son to the therapies and support him in his recovery.

Wishes do come true.

CHAPTER 4

The Diagnosis

Adam was initially funded for three hours of speech therapy a week. We began immediately after the funding was approved. Referred to an infant specialist, I loaded up the diaper bag and the baby and drove six times a week to and from the speech therapist's office for his thirty-minute sessions. She sat on the floor with lots of books and toys while Adam cried and stood by the door wanting to get out. We tried with me in the room, out of the room, having him on my lap, lying down, sitting in the car seat, jumping in the bouncer, but not one word did he say. He would cry for all thirty minutes and we would end saying, "We'll try again tomorrow." By August we figured out that this was not working. It would have been so much easier on everyone, especially Adam, if we had only stopped to ask ourselves, "Would you *really* put a two-month-old into speech therapy?" But because of the hope that the gaps between his developmental age and his chronological age could be closed, I just did not know how to even think of that question.

By the end of September, we had switched to having an in-home therapist who came to the house for two hours a week and sat with Adam at his Little Tykes table and held M&Ms in front of his face, encouraging Adam to make eye contact. Nowadays they call it ABA, and it is the most popular form of early intervention, but back in 1989, all we did was encourage a love of chocolate. Paul Coyne was a pioneer practitioner in applied behavioral analysis, based on the early works of Dr. Ivar Lovas, whose use of electric shock on individuals with intellectual delays and its effectiveness in changing behavior were highly disputed. At least we were getting away from the theories of the "refrigerator mom." But within three weeks, Dr. Coyne was not getting the results for which he had hoped, and although the word *autism* was still not said, he was the first to state that Adam's PDD was too severe to be helped. It also did not help that as part of his undergrad degree in psychology at UCLA, Adam's dad had spent a semester working with a client in Lovas's clinic, and from this expertise, he was ready to pronounce that "no way was this going to work with Adam." Silly me—reaching out to professionals.

In addition to my "someone will know someone will know someone" theory on getting help, I also have developed an understanding that "when we are ready, we will receive the information we need." From Regional Center, to the speech therapist, to sitting at the Little Tykes table with a bag of M&Ms, I learned about the ICEC (Intervention Center for Early Childhood), which, as written in their mission statement "*is dedicated to serving children who from birth to 3 years of age have developmental delays with a variety of special needs, including, but not limited to, autism, down syndrome, cerebral palsy, sensory issues, prematurity, and general developmental delays that are undiagnosed. We offer comprehensive group and individual early intervention services. Our services involve both parent participation groups and individual programs, depending upon the child's individual needs.*"

Bingo! Undiagnosed developmental delays. *Double bingo!* Funded by Regional Center. *Not so bingo!* Required parent participation.

As I look back, I ask myself why I did not simply request a family leave for the 1989–1990 school year, but equal to how I pursued doing all I could for Adam, I needed Adam's dad to also be an active participant. And so I created a plan that demanded that for this two-day-a-week parent participatory program, both Adam's dad and I would take one day a week off work so that Adam could join the ICEC. Adam's dad fought this plan with great resistance but eventually agreed, only if he could tell his district that I was undergoing chemotherapy rather than having to admit that our son was in trouble. Imagine how deep the denial was that having a wife with cancer was a story preferable to having a son with autism. By the end of November, Adam went to the ICEC on Wednesday and Friday mornings, and one of us was with him. The hardest part of taking off a day of school each week was the lesson plans we had to write, always tedious and time consuming, and to return to the classroom the next day only to discover that the lessons had not been taught anyway. At least my district did not think I was dying of cancer.

Arriving at the ICEC for the first time, my head was swirling and there was a pit in my stomach. I could hardly breathe. We had been searching, searching, testing, pushing forward to the tune of nearly $20,000, and I just did not know how to stop the momentum and settle into what would become our new normal. The anxiety came from my own denial, I suppose. The search had been so intense that I was not prepared to walk into a room with parents and children from birth to three years who were of a variety of special needs, including, but not limited to, autism, down syndrome, cerebral palsy, sensory issues, prematurity, and general developmental delays. It was not fun. After morning circle we would rotate to a variety of learning stations for speech, communication, physical and occupational therapies, music, relaxation, and massage. Parents were sitting in the opening circle, children on their laps, children crawling all over the place, children drooling, picking their noses, moms laughing, kids with hand bells. There was colorful equipment, tunnels, balls, and mats—it looked just like Gymboree. Why were these people so happy? Didn't everyone feel like I did, drained and heartsick because something was wrong with their child? I never expected to walk into the world of special education. I certainly never expected to find joy in it. But our occupational therapist, Ms. Kathy, came right over to us, gave me a hug, and said, "Oh, I have waited so long to have a kiddo like Adam." She picked up Adam, and I bolted out of the room sobbing. They were good tears, great tears—tears because for the first time since the night terrors began, I did not feel all alone.

During the three-hour sessions, we would rotate every fifteen minutes to a different station where therapists would work with the children and teach the parents how to follow through at home. It was a wonderful place full of hope and joy. The therapeutic team loved their roles, loved the children, and loved on us. Their optimism and encouragement filled me with courage and strength. We were with the ICEC for eight months, yet we saw little change in Adam. Outcomes were measured by how long he could sit in the opening circle, his enjoyment of water play and his agility in crawling through the colorful obstacle course. He did not start to speak again. And every time he was given a crayon, he would obsess on writing the letters *FHE* wherever he could.

I learned many, many things during our eight months at the ICEC. Adam went every Friday with his dad, and I took him every Wednesday. The days were divided this way because on Wednesdays there was an hour-long parent support meeting, and Adam's dad was already being asked to do more than he was emotionally ready to handle. Having to participate and share feelings at a parent support meeting would have been asking too much. I respected that; he did not want to talk with me about Adam—how could he handle sharing feelings with complete strangers? Plus I liked therapy. The parent support meetings forced me to change my understanding of the *circumstances* with my son. I was doing a great job of beating myself up regularly, trying to understand where I went wrong as mother. I labored over every moment of my pregnancy. I would watch and watch again the home videos of Adam's first year. What did I not see? My weekly contributions in the parent support group revolved around "What did I do wrong?" and "How could I have not noticed that something was wrong before it was too late?" Sadly, my fears and self doubts were reinforced by Adam's dad.

The power of being part of a group is that others hear what you say (ad infinitum), and they can respond. And after a few months of this pity party, two moms finally had had enough of me. Amy, Annie's mom, interrupted one of my self-flagellations with an abrasive "*Will you just stop it?* At least you had over a year of normal! From the moment Annie came out—we knew." Annie was a down syndrome baby; she and Amy had been coming to the ICEC since she was six weeks old. Then Connor's mom added, "You know, Sheila, I look at Adam and I see this beautiful little boy, and as far as I can tell, he is going to live a happy, healthy life." Connor had Hunter syndrome, and because a variety of complications affect the lungs, heart, joints, connective tissue, and brain and nervous system, Connor was not expected to live past the age of seven. Forever grateful to these two women—learning to appreciate the hand I had been dealt—I shut up. Deep down it would take much longer for me not see Adam as broken. I kept waiting for Pinocchio's Blue Fairy to arrive and turn him back into a real little boy.

In March 1990, a well-renowned psychiatrist from UCLA's Neuro-Psychiatric Institute would be presenting her work at a conference in Orange County and the wonderful Ms. Kathy suggested that Adam's dad and I go to this conference with her. Although we did not yet know, Ms. Kathy knew that what would be presented was what we needed to hear. Whether we were ready or not, it was time for us to hear the word. In her soothing, gentle way, Ms. Kathy would be there to hold us up at this moment of truth.

Autism.

Dr. B. J. Freeman, whose warmth and demeanor was like sharing a bowl of matzah ball soup with my favorite Aunt Sylvia, presented profile after profile of the autism spectrum—Heinz 57, and by the end of the weekend, we no longer needed to search for a diagnosis.

We knew.

Our son was autistic.

His dad went out for a walk—came back just in time for a silent drive home.

During an afternoon break, I had the opportunity to speak with Dr. Freeman. Standing by the pool at the Newport Hyatt Regency, Auntie B. J. looked at me and simply stated, "You know."

I did.

Adam was a perfect match for one of the profiles she presented. It included another Disney reference, an adorable, loveable character about which was said, "This is Dopey—he doesn't talk."

"Darling, tell me what you have gone through to get here today."

My story was not unfamiliar to her, and when I got to the part where I was told that it was my fault because I was a working mother, the renowned Dr. B. J. Freeman took my chin in her hands, forced me to have direct eye contact (must have already been force of habit), and said, "That fucking Freudian."

Just as my Aunt Sylvia would have done while chomping on a dill pickle.

She looked at me compassionately.

I cried.

Ms. Kathy held me up.

Release.

As I stood there in Ms. Kathy's arms, letting go of a year's worth of pent up fear and guilt, I saw Adam's dad standing on the second-floor balcony of the hotel, looking down at me. He was smiling.

I broke the silence on the drive home by asking him why he was up on the balcony and why he was smiling.

"I was enjoying your passion."

More silence.

March 3, 1990—the day I knew my son was autistic.

March 3, 1990—the day I knew that I was alone in this marriage.

It would take many more years until I was able to fully accept both.

I interrupt this story to tell you that although it has not been mentioned, Joshua, number 1 son, was not ignored during any of this.

As he turned two and then three, he led a wonderfully fun and active little life full of play dates and Gymboree, learning to catch and throw a ball, swimming lessons, Mommy-and-me singing groups, religious preschool, bike riding, camping, birthday parties, and family events. Everything that a growing boy deserves.

I just want to make sure that you know that he was and always will be fully loved. And loved. And loved. Once, when he was already away in college, I called him at two in the morning because I was worried that he might have felt that he did not receive enough attention. His reply? "Mom, I wish that you had not given me so much attention. I could have gotten away with more. Now go back to sleep."

I have invited Josh to write and contribute chapters of his own. As much as I want to believe that he received all that was available, there is no way that Josh's life has not been shaped by having a brother with autism. It is not easy being the "normal" child. Perhaps someday he will write a book of his own.

I hope he will.

CHAPTER 5

Welcome to the World of Special Education

September 1990—Adam entered the developmental preschool in our local school district. I wish I could report that it was a match made in heaven—that it was free from stress and tension and that the transition went well, just as we had been optimistically prepared by the ICEC staff. But what would be interesting about the first year if all had gone as we had hoped?

As promised, the school district did have an exceptional program for children with special needs. And it had the data to prove it. Every real estate agent in our city could tell you that. What I did not know was that the reason the district could boast of its remarkable outcomes was because, for lack of a better expression, they "stacked the team." None of this is to suggest that the teachers were not remarkable; they were. Nor does this mean to say that the district was not committed to being a front runner in the field; it was. In fact, there is nothing to criticize about their programs unless—unless... unless your child was as *severely* delayed/disabled as was Adam.

At our first IEP meeting with the school district for our now three-year-old son, we were told by the director of early childhood special education that we should *not* have high expectations for our son, that he most likely would never talk again, that he would always be dependent on us for everything, and that, although I was not sure why this was considered to be an important skill for a three-year-old, he would never be able to balance a checkbook. Perhaps the director of early childhood special education thought that I hoped that one day Adam would take over that task for me. I just did not know what I was hoping for. He was firm that the school district did not have a place for Adam.

Interestingly, this was the last parent conference, IEP, that this man would be conducting for the district, for he was moving on to a new position as chair of special education at one of Orange County's private universities. Hence, also joining us at our first meeting was the *new* director of early childhood special education. On one side of the table sat the director for whom Adam would be his last intake; on the other side sat the director, for whom Adam would be her first. We are just that special. And holding my hand as she had done for the past eight months was Adam's occupational therapist from the ICEC, Ms. Kathy.

There was no mistaking how horrified the new director of early childhood special education was at the cold and abrupt demeanor of her soon-to-be predecessor. She felt completely confident that Adam belonged in the school district preschool. The two of them got into it with each other, something I do not think was supposed to happen in our presence. But what did I know? This was our introduction to public school special education, and although I had heard some horror stories, those were generally about fights between the parents and the district, not the district and the district.

Now I am a teacher. And Adam's dad is also a teacher. We had a pretty good idea of how meetings were supposed to be run, having led them with our students and their parents for a combined total of seventeen years. In fact, prior to walking into the office, I was admonished by Adam's dad to remember to "let them conduct the meeting—you are the mom this time, Sheila, not the teacher." So not to embarrass Adam's dad or myself, I listened to their debate, overwhelmed by the ABCs of acronyms and mortified by the level of interaction over their disagreement. Dr. B kept saying, "SELPA, SELPA" while Dr. H replied, "He's too young for us to know. We have to give it some time."

"It's your call, Bev," said Dr. B. "You're the *new* director." *Ouch.* Then he stood up, picked up his briefcase, took the nameplate off his desk, looked at Adam's dad and me and said, "Good luck to you, folks," and excused himself.

We just sat there at the table. Silence prevailed for a moment while Dr. H collected herself. No, this definitely was *not* the appropriate protocol. Of course, it was the ever-calm, ever-wise Ms. Kathy who broke the ice. "Do you two understand what just happened here?"

Of course not. I began to cry.

"May I explain?" she calmly asked Dr. H.

"Please, thank you, yes."

It was then that I learned how the district could document such amazing success with its Special Education programs. In 1977, all school districts and county school offices in California were mandated to form consortiums in geographical regions of enough size and scope to provide for all special education service needs of children residing within the region boundaries. Each region, Special Education Local Plan Area (SELPA), developed a local plan describing how it would provide special education services. It was decided that the Orange County Department of Education would provide classes for the most medically fragile and developmentally severe students. What this meant was, as Dr. B was recommending, that the district special education program did not have to accept Adam and that he should be sent to the county program. In sum, the school district did not have to keep data on these most severe students because they were not part of the district. It allowed the district to report its successes with the students who were most likely to succeed. What this meant to Dr. H was that keeping Adam in the district program would save the school district tens of thousands of dollars each year, for it was the district who would have to foot the bill if Adam were sent to the county program. My god, Adam was but a few weeks past his third birthday and he was already being edged out of the highly coveted "most likely to succeed" in his high school yearbook, circa 2005. What about the family legacy? No, wait, I was voted "most school spirit"—never mind. With Dr. B out of the room, the new director of preschool special education found her voice. "How about we start over?" she asked most pleasantly.

By the end of the meeting it was decided that Adam would start in the special education preschool in our local school because his teacher was to be Ms. T, who had taught in the county program for many years prior to transferring to the district. Certainly, according to Dr. H, with Ms. T we had the best fit possible. And then, there was that little caveat, that was not formally written into the IEP, but rather spoken, softly, as a mere suggestion, an aside—perhaps in quiet deference to the departing director. Since Ms. T was going to have her first baby in February and would be taking her maternity leave at the end of January, perhaps, *just in case things didn't work out*, we should meet again at the end of the first semester and hear Ms. T's recommendation on what would be best for Adam. Ms. Kathy thought this sounded reasonable, and so did Adam's dad. Honestly, I was still stuck on balancing the checkbook.

I left the meeting not knowing whether it had been a successful one. Yes, Adam had been accepted by the elite district. The preschool he would attend at Los Naranjos (the Oranges) was well-known as an exemplary model of inclusion—half typical and half special education students back in the days before *inclusion* became part of mainstream educational jargon. The IEP allotted two hours a week for speech therapy, three hours a week for sensory integration therapy, a weighted vest, and a trampoline. The reason that my head was spinning was due to the special education vocabulary, abbreviations, and acronyms. I mean, I had taken the required special education classes as part of my teaching credential, even though I knew that I would *never* be needing *that* information; after all, I was going to be a drama teacher, so why did I need to pay attention to those terms? And yet here I was, needing all that information and more. I kept wondering, *if this is so difficult for me to understand, what about all the parents who do not have a background in education?* And what about parents who do not speak English but have a child with special needs? And what about the families who do not live in our model city? I knew that our journey with Adam could not just be about the journey with Adam, that I had a responsibility to take all that I had been learning and share it with others. I wanted to be one of the people who was someone who knew someone who knew someone who knew someone so that I could help make all this easier on another family. That's just who I am.

But back to the story, on Thursday, September 6, 1990, Adam had his first day of school at Los Naranjos.

That first semester flew by. Not as planned, but indeed, the months flew by. During the summer of 1989, we had moved to the neighborhood for which Los Naranjos was the neighborhood school. I was certain that I would be walking Adam to school at seven forty-five each morning for the eight o'clock bell, and then I would run home, get in my car, and drive to my school to teach my first class. With the support of my wonderful department chair, I had been scheduled to teach without having a conference period, 9:00 a.m.–2:00 p.m. and then hop back in the car to pick up Adam at 2:30 p.m. The preschool was out at 1:45 p.m., but Easter Seals held an after-school program right at Los Naranjos, so Adam would have nap time in the day care room. *Perfect.*

Oh no.

At the IEP, we learned that the start of the school day had been changed to 8:30 a.m. and those thirty minutes, those dirty thirty minutes changed everything. So much for my plan. For me to get to my school on time, I would put Adam in my car and drive the five and a half miles from our home, where at 7:45 a.m. we would meet the little yellow school bus on the corner of Yale and Meadow Wood so that Adam could get on the little yellow school bus and ride back the five and a half miles to our neighborhood. I kid you not.

The speech therapy was part of his school day, and on Monday, Tuesday, and Thursday afternoons at 4:00 p.m., we would go to sensory integrative therapy where he would twist and turn and bounce and play in hopes of resetting his proprioceptive balance in the world. I was such a supermom. I would get up at 4:45 a.m., run six miles, get home, shower and get dressed, do my five-minute makeup, wake up the boys, get them dressed, give them breakfast, take Josh to Ms. Linda's at 7:30 a.m., and get to the bus stop at Yale and Meadow Wood by 7:45 p.m. Yeah, baby! I could do it all!

I believed that Adam was welcomed and adored by all. He was cute. He was adorable. He was affectionate. He was cooperative. He wanted to learn. And he loved books; yes indeed, he loved books. Except for the fact that he did not talk, there was hardly a noticeable difference between Adam and the other three-year-olds. Well, except for those *autistic things*—like he did not talk, he threw tantrums, he hit himself on the head and bit his finger, he needed to wear the weighted vest several times a day, and he would not stay with the group. Other than that, you could hardly tell he was different. He had communication goals, academic goals, recreational goals, physical goals, occupational goals, and social goals, all of which were designed to either eliminate or modify behaviors. No matter how much his teacher and the aides loved him, there was not a goal written that would make the autism go away. And all along, they knew (although I did not) that when Ms. T left on maternity leave, so would Adam.

Ms. T was indeed an outstanding teacher, and as January drew near and she was about to go on leave to have her baby, she started to prepare us for the reality that without her at the helm of the ship; there was not another preschool teacher with the depth and breadth of experience she had working with young children with autism. She explained where and how and why the district was not meeting Adam's needs. We needed to go visit the county program.

The unknown is always the scariest. Way back in high school, my psychology class had visited Fairview Developmental Center, a state institute where the most severely disabled were housed. And in college when I took that class in mainstreaming and had to pass tests on all that "stuff" that I knew that I would never need to use in my classroom, we had to attend a dance at Lanterman Center, another state institution for the severely disabled. These visits were before the ADA was signed into legislation and only a few had heard the term "least restrictive environment." My fear of the county program came from the memories of a seventeen-year-old high school student and a twenty-one-year-old college student working on her credential, who had not been emotionally mature enough to interact with adults who wore helmets and diapers and drooled. All I could imagine was that my beautiful three-year-old son would be in a school that was dank and smelled of ammonia. You bet I was scared and filled with distress. I just did not know what it would look like. And pressure, so much pressure from parents in our autism support group. "Fight it—fight for your son. It's his right to stay in the preschool you want. We have a lawyer for you. Do not let them bully you into this. You're the mom—you know what is best." I was immobilized by the fear and anxiety.

That same year was the first time that a student with autism had been placed in my Drama I class. Steven J. loved to watch movies, so his IEP team thought that maybe he might love to learn how to be an actor. Now drama kids are very loving and accepting; after all, they are already the weirdest kids in the school—on the C-list of popularity at best. And the kids did welcome Steven J. into our class with enthusiasm. But the disparity between my adorable son at the age of three and other three-year-olds, and a sixteen-year-old adolescent full of hormones and juices and his high school peers, forced me to look at Adam's future. Talk about a flash-forward. Steven's mom begged us to keep him in class after he was found masturbating at the back of the theater, and it was heartbreaking when we had our stagecraft unit and I just could not allow him to work the jigsaw—it wasn't on the IEP. But it was when he came bounding at me with the claw-tooth hammer, I understood he was really frustrated, and I was not safe. Mom came down to school again in tears. Too close to home. Too close to my heart. From Steven J. and his mom during that same semester when my own son with autism was in the "least restrictive environment," I learned what proved to be the most valuable question to ask "Whose needs are we meeting here?" Yes, more than anything, I want my son to be *normal*, whatever that means, this coming from the teacher who was the best person to be leading all those special and unique drama kids for the obvious reasons. And as we went to visit the "county program" for the first time, I promised myself that I would look at the program through the eyes of a mother unlike Steven J.'s mother, who, in loving her son so very, very much, wanted him to be so *normal* that he was placed in a drama class because she had loved her drama classes when she was in high school. When Steven J was removed from my drama class for being a danger to other students, I felt like I had failed him tremendously, and I do not know who ached more—his mom or me. And because of her anger at her circumstances, she threatened to sue the school district and me. As both an observer and a participant in her dreams, hopes, and pain as her son, Steven J., could not find a place to fit in, I learned that I had to be willing to accept Adam for who he is—not who I hoped he would be.

Life's teachers show up when we need them most.

With strong urging from Ms. T, who was clearly advocating for my son's greater needs, it was time for us look at the county program. I first had to confront my grief that Adam was being rejected and hence ejected from the district preschool. My heart ached with tremors; how can a three-year-old be kicked out of a program? And not just any three-year-old, *my* adorable, sweet, precious, autistic three-year-old? Step two was to come to terms with the lessons from Mrs. J, from whom I learned to ask, whose need would I be meeting if I fought for Adam to stay at Los Naranjos. Step three was to ponder if I was I strong enough to fight the district. I was so grateful that I did not teach in the same district in which my children were enrolled, for there was no way I could have taken on my own employer. In contrast, step four necessitated that I be strong enough to endure the criticism of the parents of autistic children who were counting on me to join them in waging legal battles against school districts, demanding that their sons and daughters be mainstreamed. How could I go against my own tribe of parents who had been dealing with this far longer than me? It meant that I had to be very, very courageous, honest, and objective when considering the most important factor, *what would truly be the best for Adam?*

These many years later, I am happy to be able to share that all my fears of the county program were for naught. For starters, back to the SELPA we had heard about last summer, the county classes were housed in the local school district as part of the regular school campuses. Adam would be in our home district until the age of eighteen, at which point, he would enter a transitional program closest to our home. He would be given opportunities to be integrated each day into regular education classes with a one-on-one teacher's aide. The 12:1 ratio of the school district program was reduced to 6:1 at the country program, so he would receive more individual attention/instruction. Every teacher was also a certified behaviorist so that in addition to the outside therapy services that would continue, every interaction would have integrated support. Oh, one thing more—the county program started at 8:00 a.m., so I could drive Adam to school myself and he could go to Koala Kids, in the classroom right next door at the end of the school day. To my surprise, Adam enjoyed riding the bus more! So he was picked up right in front of our house at 7:40 a.m., and we no longer had to drive to the intersection of Yale and Meadow Wood. Thus began our eighteen-year relationship with Laidlaw Bus Company, who never once let us down.

On the emotional side, the principal, teachers, specialists, and instructional assistants who taught in the county program were so happy to welcome Adam. There was no whispering this time *just in case it didn't work out.* It clearly was where my son belonged and where, as we would consistently experience, he would grow and thrive.

From February 1991 to June 2009, Adam attended what I believe to be the finest educational program that he could have possibly received. He did begin to talk and communicate. He learned to read and write and do math. We even figured out what FHE was all about. He made friends, attended parties, learned to swim, and played baseball and soccer. He got a job. And yes, Adam did learn to balance a check book. Actually, he is a genius with numbers! Through the remarkable educational opportunities provided by the Autism Program at the Orange County Department of Education, Adam was given a path for his future.

And then I blinked.

It was 2009, and at twenty-two, Adam was ready to graduate from OCDE special programs. That June, just before graduation, I was invited to speak on a parent panel as the "graduating parent." Over 250 teachers, specialists, and para-pros from OCDE were in attendance. I began my talk by requesting, "Will anyone here who has ever worked with my son over the past nineteen years please stand?" Over half the room rose. The number of people standing was daunting. From his earliest teacher in the preschool to his transition teacher and job coaches at Orange Coast College, they were all there. These people had held both my son's and my hands through every transition, every life event, every up and down, every IEP meeting, every challenge, every success and disappointment imaginable. The only people not in the room that afternoon who deserved as much gratitude and thanks were those Laidlaw bus drivers, who for nineteen years had safely driven my son to and from school, greeting him each day with a "Good morning, Adam," and sending him off in the afternoon with a cheerful "See you tomorrow!" These remarkable, selfless people were our village. Better yet, they were our marines, for it took the best of the best to help me raise my son. And they did.

Some of you may be hoping that we experienced a miracle and that Adam was *cured*. That the Blue Fairy came down and made him into a "real little boy."

He is still autistic and always will be.

But we did have our miracle—the miracle of working with hundreds of remarkable people who dedicate their lives as educators to improve the lives of those children, who to most, seem hopeless. They were our

"Collective Blue Fairy." The miracles that this group of educators performed, and it took many, many years for me to accept, was that they helped me to know that my son was never broken.

I have sat on both sides of the table as a parent and as a teacher. The stack of IEPs for my own son stands over four feet tall—a lot of goals were written over nineteen years. And since Steven J., many more students with autism were placed in my drama classes. I have been lauded as being an exceptional parent (which I am not) and have been taken to court by parents suing a district for not meeting their child's needs (which I did). I have experienced the full gamut and more times than not, I have gone back to what I learned in that first special education class in college, all that stuff I never expected to use as a teacher and certainly not as a parent. To paraphrase the brilliant Joni Mitchell, "*I've looked at autism from both sides now, from up and down, and still somehow, it's autism illusions I recall, I really don't know autism at all*" (Mitchell, Joni, "Both Sides Now," 1967).

But here is what I do know, and I will not be very popular for saying this. But say it I must.

What is all this talk I hear of sorrow and weariness, anger, discontent and drooping hopes? Parents! *You* are the first and most important teachers in your child's life. Yes, you are hurt and fearful and angry at the cards you have been dealt, but it is *your* responsibility to find gratitude and joy in what is provided for our children rather than channeling your heartbreak into lawsuits and unrealistic expectations. Accept your child for who he is. Love her for the many experiences and people you would have never met had it not been for her. *Autism is too strong for you. It takes autism to love autism* (Masters, Edgar Lee, *Spoon River Anthology*, "Lucinda Matlock," 1916).

This is our life, our journey, and I sure do love my tour guide.

There are many, many stories to tell.

Read on.

CHAPTER 6

Dr. Looney

I did not like to talk about or focus on the difficult times. I figured that after surviving the night terror years, it would be healthier to move forward and forget that we were exhausted and consumed by them. Besides, Adam's dad was insistent that we never let anyone in the outside world know that we were struggling—that our public persona must be one of patience and grace so that no one would ever question that we were not surviving raising a child with autism. Heck, even at the autism conferences, where other parents would be sure to specify that their child was "high functioning," we were the pariahs who silently nodded and smiled never admitting that our son was low functioning. No one wanted to associate with a family like ours, not even those whose children were labeled Aspergers. Perhaps we were striving to convince ourselves that we were handling life so well, despite the stresses we felt day in and day out. But the reality was that as Adam turned four, then five, and was soon approaching six, there were times when his behaviors were so out of control, and we just did not know what to do. It became our norm, and we just pretended that we knew exactly how to handle whatever came our way. Everything was fine, just fine.

We kept plodding along like a "normal" family, as normal as a family can be who always travels in two cars, deals with violent tantrums in the grocery story, has lost most of their friends, and is doing their best, as Bozo said, to "always keep laughing." We were living in a circus.

Ha! Ha! Ha!

And we were not allowed to complain; that would have been a Big Bozo no-no!

People who did not know, as well as those who did not know better, would approach us out of nowhere and say the damnedest things. Once at the grocery store, after having observed an Adam meltdown over…who knows what…possibly his frustration at not being able to tell us what kind of cereal he wanted us to get for him, an older woman came up to our cart shaking her finger at Adam, saying, "You are a very, very bad boy." I tried to wheel us away, but she kept following us, "And you are a very, very bad mother." This was before I found my voice in knowing how to respond. Today I would tactlessly say something like, "My son is autistic. What the fuck is your problem?"

The stress had begun to take its toll on Josh as well. It was not easy having a brother who acts so weird; "What's wrong with your brother?" his squeaky voiced pals would ask. "How come your brother makes those noises?" And even the other second-grade parents were reluctant to let their sons have a sleepover at our house. "Does Adam ever have problems during the night?" they would hesitantly inquire. It was not an unreasonable question; after all, they may have been at Josh's school the day Adam melted down in the Alderwood Library, or they may have seen him freak out when we walked past a dry cleaner. Where other families made a weekly ritual to Costco on a Sunday morning to enjoy free samples, the humming fluorescent lights in the warehouse were too painful for Adam to handle, so Josh and I had to miss tasting the apple strudel, blueberry yogurt, or chocolate-chunk cookies that were being handed out. During his second-grade year, Josh was asked to draw a picture of our family, and he did not include Adam in the drawing. Needless to say I was distressed and worried and immediately sought out a support group for Josh, something along the lines of a *group for the brothers and sisters, the perfect sibling in the family, where the demands of the child with the disability require so much more time, attention and energy even when the parents are in denial that there is anything wrong in the family"* or something like that. The wonderful Ms. Kathy from the ICEC had just completed her MFCC, and because she is the wonderful Ms. Kathy, she ran with the idea and Josh became the first member of her sibling support group. You can well imagine Adam's dad's reaction to my seeking a therapeutic support group for Josh. "Why do you have to make both of our children wrong?" he lamented. "Do not tell anyone, especially my family." Once again, the only thing wrong within our family was my inadequacy as a mother. Nothing new. Same old, same old.

Another area in our lives that was affected was that we were no longer welcome at our synagogue. We had been one of the first families to become members of our synagogue in 1986, but to show up with a child diagnosed with a severe disability two years later, well, even within our spiritual community, no one knew what to say to us. We were trend setters having a child with autism, the first to pave the way for the explosion to come. Who knew? But where I was once hopeful that at least here we would not be shunned, it was yet another area of our lives where we lost a part of the life we had once lived. I do not blame anyone; everyone was as bewildered as we were. "You are so strong," people would say. "He is so cute. He doesn't look like anything is wrong with him." And of course, my favorite platitude, "God won't give you anything you can't handle." Are you kidding me? What kind of god sends a child with autism into a family to handle? When Adam was four years old, one Shabbat morning at the religious school book fair, when I could not understand what Adam wanted, he magnetically fell to the ground in full autistic meltdown, me struggling to pick him up to get him to the car. Amid Adam's screaming and kicking legs, as other parents and their kids circled round watching the circus, even the rabbi came outside to see what was happening. All the lookie-loos, who stared at us in horror, were poised, ready to watch the rabbi perform a miracle. But the best this man could say to me in solace and comfort was "Sheila, have you ever considered putting him in a home?" No miracle; we Jews hadn't seen one of those since the burning bush. Adam was six years old; was the Rabbi fucking kidding me?

However, within the congregation members who came running out to see the spectacle of our lives was the wonderful Dr. Marc Lerner, who happened to be a pediatric specialist, a pioneer in working with children with autism at University California Irvine. We knew the Lerner family socially through synagogue life, and they were one of the few families who still invited us to do things with them—Marc being a specialist in autism and all.

I had not considered the option of taking Adam to Marc professionally for three reasons: first, after that first experience with Dr. C at UCI, I was afraid to go back there; second, our insurance did not cover UCI and we were still paying off bills from the diagnostic year; and third, I did not want to take advantage of Dr. Lerner. After all, we had so few people willing to be our friends anymore. In this instance, I was completely wrong.

While the Rabbi was on the sidelines urging me to put Adam into a group home, Dr. Lerner calmly walked over to us, and using his experience with children with autism, he picked up Adam, soothed his soul, and carried him to the car. Once inside the safety and privacy of our 1989 blue-gray Dodge Caravan, I was the one who had the meltdown. I was so ashamed that anyone, *anyone*, would see me crying in public. No one gets to know how hard this is. I did not know how I would tell Adam's dad about what had happened. It was just more evidence that I was a very, very bad mother. Dr. Lerner sat in the passenger's seat as I regained my composure. "Sheila, I want you to bring Adam over to the clinic."

"But-but-but—" I stammered.

"We have been waiting for you for two years."

"But I do not want to take advantage of you."

"Tell you what. You take advantage of me now, and when Emily and Dori are in high school, Karen and I will take advantage of you."

The agreement was made.

Two weeks later we were in Dr. Lerner's office at UCI. There really was not much for him to examine, for he had been watching Adam's development from afar just as he said, "For the past two years." While we talked, his assistant, Winnie, kept Adam engaged with puzzles and shapes as she tried to coax language out of him. "Sheila," Dr. Lerner asked me, "Have you ever considered putting Adam on some medications?" Now *that* was a potent question.

My first pregnancy was during the years when we were all about "natural childbirth." Learning to breath in, breath out, breath in, breath out, watch your focal point—relax, relax, relax.

And even though it hurt, painfully, "*Help! Bring me the drugs!*" by the time I dilated to four centimeters, I was still deeply impacted by Nancy Regan's "Just say no" campaign, as much as it could relate to pregnant women. I felt a deep sense of failure when I was unable to push that baby out and had to have an emergency C-section, and even more so when my husband's twin brother told me, "You could have gotten him out if you had only tried harder." Yes, I was labeled as a failure as a mother even during delivery. It is no wonder that I was confused and uncertain about putting my six-year-old son on drugs.

"Tell me your concerns," he said.

Sigh. "Well, Adam's dad feels that meds are a copout. He sees so many of his students taking meds, and he says it is because their parents are lazy. And I do not want to be a lazy mom. I want to be sure that we are doing all we can for Adam before we make a decision like this."

Dr. Lerner nodded. "I understand."

He paused, waiting to hear what I might say next. I just looked at the pictures of the happy families hanging on the wall of the office.

"Marc," I asked, "do you think I will ever feel happy again?"

"I don't know," he replied. "It's a good question. You know, you carry a lot of burdens. All parents with autistic children do."

I nodded, avoiding eye contact.

Adam and Winne continued to play on the other side in the observation room.

"He's a happy, boy, Sheila. Look at him."

We did.

"But it's not this way at home, is it? Truthfully, you can tell me. It's the only way I can know if I can help."

Our lovely home, the one that was so near to Los Naranjos, the school which Adam attended for four and a half short months now had holes in the walls from Adam's tantrums. We would plaster them up, but within a few days, new ones would appear. The family room carpet was stained with the letters *FHE* written in felt pen, some large, some small, and no matter how many times we tried, no carpet cleaner would get them out. We did not know what they meant. *FHE* was also written all over the walls in Adam's bedroom, the boys' bathroom and the garage floor. FHE. FHE. FHE.

"Does he kick the walls?"

"Yes."

"Does he hit his head?"

"Often," I whispered.

How many extra locks do you have on the doors, so he won't go out in the middle of the night?"

I counted. "Total? Seven."

I looked at Adam playing so calmly with Winnie. Calm for other people, not for me.

And then Dr. Lerner presented three options for me to consider—about the medication.

I am an "all or nothing" thinker. It never occurred to me that there might be options to consider. Dr. Lerner presented a new way of seeing things that in my overwhelming feelings of motherhood failure, I would have never known were possible.

"So what I would recommend for Adam would be to start him on a low dose of Risperdal. And we wait to see what happens."

I listened.

"One of three things will happen and then you can decide. One, he will take the Risperdal, and nothing will happen. Two, he will take the Risperdal, and you will like what happens. Three, he will take the Risperdal and you will not like what happens, so we take him off."

I had to work hard to block out the voice of Adam's dad, "Only lazy parents put their kids on meds."

And then Dr. Lerner, because he is Dr. Lerner, said something that no one else had ever said before. "As your doctor, it is my responsibility not only to treat Adam but to treat the entire family. And, Sheila, your family is in trouble. You deserve to have some peace in your lives."

I was so grateful for that conversation. It was the first time I had stopped in well over four years to barely consider myself. Autism had consumed my life. Motherhood had consumed my life. Being a wife had consumed my life. Teaching had consumed my life. Family had consumed my life. Soccer, PTA, essays to grade, and trying to please the world had consumed my life. "My family was in trouble and we deserved some peace in our lives."

For the second time in our journey with Adam, I made the unpopular decision in the eyes of the other parents in our autism support group—Adam was going try the meds. While other parents were having their autistic children swimming with the dolphins or flying to Paris to have their inner ear calibrated with a tuning fork, both of which had sworn testimony would make the autism go away, I took the lazy parent's way out and followed Dr. Lerner's advice. After all, he had given me permission to know that with option 3: "We could always take him off."

Our next hurdle was getting Adam to take the medicine. He refused to swallow the little yellow pill. We ground it up and put it in a medicine dropper, squeezing his cheeks closed so he would swallow. It all came hurling out at us. Crushed up in fruit juice, ice cream, apple sauce? His taste buds told him, "No, no, no." We felt so devious, manipulative, and conniving trying to get him to take the Risperdal for weeks with no success. And then Dr. Lerner told us that one of his families was having success putting it into macaroni and cheese. Bingo! The miraculous cheese covered both the color and the taste, and Adam happily ate macaroni and cheese twice a day. This was still years before the popular belief became that autism would disappear through a nondairy, nongluten diet—and by the time these theories and practices were introduced, Adam had long been taking his pills with water.

It was not long before Teacher Pat from Meadowpark Elementary reported that Adam was much calmer during the school day. And within two months, he had begun to talk. We were able to change insurance companies, and as much as I had feared taking advantage of Dr. Lerner, he assured me that he would be on Adam's team for the rest of his life as needed. Way past the pediatric age of eighteen. He also made me promise to take care of myself and find some peace.

Adam had long been memorizing everything he heard, not necessarily the words and their meanings, but the phonetic quality of the sounds. His best teachers were Dr. Seuss, Disney songs, Peter, Paul, and Mary and his favorite, a group called Parachute Express, a lively and colorful trio who wrote all the music for *Gymboree*. Steven, Donnie and Janis were staples in our home on tape, later CD, and then video. We traveled to see them live in concert and during that hour and a half, Adam was just as delighted as every other child dancing and singing to their songs. This was a joyfully normal event for both Joshua and Adam.

We would visit Dr. Lerner every few months to check on Adam's meds and for Dr. Lerner to check on us. Even though we had a scheduled appointment, sometimes, well, most of the time, Dr. Lerner ran late. Not a criticism; he was kind and generous with the time and attention he gave to every family, just as I knew he would be with us. Indeed, as promised, he treated the entire family. Waiting, however, was not one of Adam's finer qualities, so our routine was to drive around the UCI parking lot listening to Parachute Express music until Winnie would come outside to wave us in. Today we would text. But it was 1995 and the best we had was a pager. Sometimes Adam would refuse to go in, so Dr. Lerner would come out to the car, the same blue-gray Dodge van he had carried Adam to many years before. And sometimes we would casually stroll into his office. Adam's keen sense always knew when it was a day for inoculations, and these visits were not particularly fun. Four of Dr. Lerner's staff and I would hold Adam down just long enough for the shot to be administered. Autism did not affect Adam's strength at all. Under certain conditions, he became the Incredible Hulk.

At Dr. Lerner's office, no one came up to Adam to tell him that he was a "very, very bad boy," nor did anyone ever tell me that I was a "very, very bad parent." We were being treated as a family. Which is why on one afternoon Adam put everything in perfect perspective. Sitting on the exam table, sticking out his tongue to say "Ah!" and having his reflexes tested with a tap on the knees, Adam began to sing one of his favorite Parachute Express songs:

> *Doctor, Doctor, better get here fast*
> *I don't think my mom will last*
> *Her tummy is filled with butterflies*
> *She's a bundle of nerves; she laughs, she cries*
> *Woah! Woah!* **Doctor Looney**, *will you fix her up?*
> (https://www.youtube.com/watch?v=HVPEAAPCld8)

I knew the words; Adam and I had sung them together hundreds of times. This was the day that I realized that I had begun to 'speak Adam. He knew exactly what he meant—and I began to interpret. Never again would I think he was perseverating on senseless words.

And that is how Dr. Lerner became Dr. Looney, who since that day has remained a revered member of Team Adam, where he shall remain for the rest of our lives.

> *Woah! Woah! Doctor Looney, will you fix us up?*
> *Woah! Woah! Woah!*

Dr. Looney's Remedy! Good for the whole family!

CHAPTER 7

Forgive Me, Son, for I Have Sinned

About the time that Josh drew the family picture sans Adam, we started to observe some other changes in his behavior. Josh was attending weekly sessions with Ms. Kathy's sibling support group, and although she wouldn't tell us everything they talked about (patient-therapist confidentiality), Ms. Kathy did keep reminding me that "it is not easy being the 'perfect' child," in other words, the one without the disability.

One of the changes in Josh was that he would only wear green and wanted us to call him Tommy. My son's first crush was on the Green Power Ranger, and he wanted to be just like him. Josh actually believed he WAS the Green Ranger. It was also the year that his soccer coach discovered that Josh was ambidextrous with his feet—he could kick a goal with either foot and was able to deceive the goalie. As Josh set up the ball for the goal, he'd fake out the goalie by starting with the right foot, but at the last moment, change it up to the left—SCORE! While Coach Dave began to call him Golden Foot, his teammates and the opposition on the field would call him "the kid with the weird brother." Josh began having some troubles at school, insisting that his teacher, Mrs. W, "hated" him. He would come home with stories of being sent into the hallway or having his work ridiculed by his teacher. After he would tell us his tale of woe, I would ask, "Josh, if Mrs. W were here, what would she tell me?" He would stomp off in anger accusing me of "taking her side." So yes, Dr. Looney was right. Everyone in our family was affected by autism, and after battling with Adam to take his meds, I did not have the focus or energy to give Josh the attention and patience that he needed. I was too quick to pop into "teacher mode" rather than being a loving and nurturing mom when my eight-year-old was crying for attention too.

My "parenting bottom" happened on a Tuesday night in February 1993. I call it "The Curious Incident of Macaroni in the Night." Once we found that we could grind his yellow Risperdal tablet and hide it in macaroni and cheese, macaroni and cheese was what Adam had for dinner—every night. It was the path of least resistance for Adam, but in our quest to get it right with at least one child, we foolishly demanded that Josh eat the well-balanced meal that the "adults" were eating for dinner. Once a month, Adam's dad and I would spend a Sunday evening preparing a month's worth of meals that we would divide up into portions and freeze. We would select five or six recipes, prepare a triple portion, and divvy them up so that in the mornings before we left for school, we would take something out of the freezer and after our long days of teaching, soccer practice, religious school, or all of Adam's therapy appointments, all we had to do was prepare a salad, a side dish, and heat up the main meal. We enjoyed planning, shopping, and working in the kitchen together and each month added one or two new recipes to our menu. *Good Housekeeping Magazine*'s meal planner had nothing on us. But nothing we prepared, nothing, seemed as yummy to Josh as did Adam's macaroni and cheese.

For months, we battled the same conversation during dinner.

"Why do I have to eat your food? Why does Adam always get to eat what *he* wants? How come *I* never get to have what *I* want? I hate this food. *It's not fair. It's not fair!*"

Josh was right—it was not fair. It was not fair that we had to deal with autism every moment of our lives. It was not fair that Adam could not function without his meds. It was not fair that we were tired, exhausted. It was not fair that Josh had to live in such chaos. It was not fair that we did not really know what we were doing. It was not fair that life was so hard. And it was not fair that I was not allowed to share how hard it was.

None of this was fair. Josh was absolutely correct.

And the role of the mean parent always fell to me.

I would try to reason with Josh, explaining that we just wanted him to learn to enjoy different, healthy foods.

"How come I have to if Adam doesn't?"

I was stubborn. As much as I could accept and take the path of least resistance with Adam, I was too rigid and stubborn with Josh. Deep down I believed that *if* I could get Josh to simply appreciate and enjoy the meals we had prepared, *then* I would know that I was being a good mother. We're Jewish—of course everything comes down to food.

I always thought that Josh would be a math/science guy like his dad even though his joys and interests were more aligned with mine. He had loved dressing up in costumes and performing full-scale one-man musicals since he was two. Yep, he was a theater kid, and like his mom, he had no difficulty expressing full-blown emotions. This meant two things: one, when it came to being stubborn, he was my equal; and two, he knew exactly how to push my buttons. He may have inherited my talent, but he also inherited his father's ability to strategize. Put those two qualities together, and we had a very brilliant son. It was that Tuesday night in February 1993 that Josh figured out what to say, the one thing that would break me emotionally and push me over the edge so that I would give in to macaroni and cheese.

Dinner was on the table, and as if on cue, the conversation began:

"Why do I have to eat your food? Why does Adam always get to eat what *he* wants? How come *I* never get to have what *I* want? I hate Chinese food."

But tonight, instead of whining "*It's not fair. It's not fair!*" Josh played this card: "*I want to be autistic!*"

And so I capitulated into action, and I gave Josh macaroni and cheese for dinner. "Victory," my older son gloated, but although it was one small step for macaroni equality, it was the gauntlet I needed to dig myself in more deeply.

All went silent at the dinner table. Even Adam sensed something was up. My mind flashed to the scene in the movie *A Christmas Story* when Ralphie says the F-word. But unlike Ralphie's mom, I did not scream, I did not fret, and I did not even grimace. After a moment's pause, I stood up from the table, picked up Joshua's plate, looked him in the eye, and made sure that I heard him correctly. "You want to be autistic?" I calmly repeated.

With fear in his eyes but confidence in his voice, he replied, "Yes."

I put his plate in the sink, took a clean bowl from the cupboard, filled it with the remaining macaroni and cheese from the pot, walked back to the table, set the bowl in front of Josh, and with continued composure said, "Okay, from now on, you are autistic."

I sat back down at our table made for four. Eyes darted back and forth. There was silence at the table.

Josh was not completely sure if he should eat the macaroni and cheese.

I began eating my dinner as if nothing was different.

"So how was your day?" I asked the boys' dad.

Still suspicious, Josh began to eat the highly coveted macaroni and cheese.

We ate in silence.

"Oh, excuse me a moment, I have to make a phone call."

I do not know where the inspiration came from. And what is even more remarkable, it was one of the few times in my life that I did not feel an early onset of remorse for what I was about to do. There was a peaceful calm in me as I got up from the table and walked to the phone. (Please note that this was years before cell phones were our constant companions. Our push button phone with the twenty-foot curly cord still hung on the wall.)

I pretended to dial and waited.

"Hello, Coach Dave? Hi, this is Sheila, Josh's mom. I am so sorry to tell you this, but Josh will not be able to play soccer anymore...

Well, he's autistic now…Yeah, not on the all-star team either…Yes, we are sorry too…Thank you. Buh-bye."

I sat back down at the table and continued to eat my dinner. More silence.

Then again, "Oh, excuse me a moment, I have to make another phone call."

I pretended to dial and waited.

"Hello, Mrs. Bletsacker? Hi, this is Sheila, Josh's mom… I am sorry to tell you this, but Josh will not be able to come to Brandon's birthday party on Sunday. Well, he's autistic now, so he does not have friends anymore… Yes, we are sorry too… Thank you… Bye-bye."

By the time I got up to make the third phone call, Josh had begun to wail, "I don't want to be autistic anymore."

It hadn't taken long to make my point.

I grabbed him up and held him as tightly as I could. Together we cried through this.

"I know this is not fair, honey, it is not fair to any of us. But mostly, it is not fair to Adam. Do you know how much he looks up to you? How much he wants to be like you? If he could, he would be the one to cry, 'My life is not fair.' You get to do so much, and you have friends, and wow—you even get to go to summer camp. There is nothing like this for Adam. Nothing. Sweetie, I know that none of this seems fair. But *fair* does not mean equal. You and Adam do not need the same things. *Fair* means that *you* get what you need, and Adam gets what *he* needs. Daddy and I try very, very hard to give you both what you need. Adam needs to eat macaroni and cheese every night for dinner because it is the only way that we can get him to take his medicine. And you need to wear green every day and want us to call you Tommy."

"I AM Tommy," he bemoaned.

Josh got it; he is smart and aware, and despite the rare moments when he acts like an overindulged seven-year-old, he figures things out quickly.

"You really didn't make those calls, did you, Mommy?"

"Of course not, and I am so sorry that I pretended to do that to you. I am so sorry, my love."

As I have written, I do not know what inspired me to do this cruel thing nor for what I was about to do next. And what was even more remarkable was that for the second time that evening, I did not feel remorse for what I was about to do to my son. There was a peaceful calm in me as I got up from the couch and went upstairs to get a notebook. (Please note this was before the days that we would have done this on the computer.)

I invited Josh over to the couch to sit close to me and cuddle, and I handed him the notebook and a pen.

"Honey, please listen to this very carefully, very carefully, for I may never acknowledge this again." I took a deep breath.

"With me as your mom, there is no doubt that you are going to need major therapy by the time you are thirty. So starting tonight, I want you to write anything down that I do that upsets you. This way, when you are thirty and you see that therapist for the first time, all you will have to do is read the list. This way, you will never need to wonder about all of the ways I have damaged you."

November 7, 2015. Josh turned thirty. While we were celebrating at a birthday lunch, he pulled out that notebook I had given him so many years ago. Guess what he read to me that day?

Nothing.

He never wrote anything down.

The day I gave him permission to document my failings as a mother, he decided he never would. Somehow, he understood that I was doing the best I could.

And you already know what he ordered for lunch—a large bowl of macaroni and cheese!

CHAPTER 8

All the Adams in the World

Despite the many cognitive and emotional delays caused by the autism, one thing that was not affected was Adam's physical development. In fact, it was the one "normal" aspect of my son. He grew taller and stronger and met the physical milestones of childhood like every growing boy, including visits from the tooth fairy. I do not remember any trauma when his first tooth fell out—nor the second or the third. Most likely, there was so much else going on that we did not have time to focus on whether or not Adam had a reaction to this natural part of childhood. He did, however, completely flip out when the time came to visit the dentist for the first time.

In 1994, Adam was seven years old.

Dr. Lovenger was highly regarded and recommended as *"the dentist"* for Adam to see. He was a pediatric specialist in the world of dentistry for children with special needs. It was a four-month wait to get in to see him, the need for this specialty so great in the Orange County area. One of the benefits of being part of the county autism program was that we and our son had access to the names and resources of people who worked with children like Adam. It was hard not to bemoan those first years when we went from doctor to doctor to doctor trying to get a diagnosis. Now, we were part of a network, and I believe that this saved us months of time, of trial and error, and I felt so grateful, for I knew this special dentist was worth the wait.

All the moms praised Dr. Lovenger for his understanding, compassion, and patience. They praised his staff for their understanding, compassion, and patience as well. In honor of Adam's seventh birthday, we scheduled his first dental appointment.

Dr. Lovenger's practice was on the second floor of the office building in Mission Viejo. Adam loved riding in elevators, so we made it up to the second floor with ease. No sooner had we exited the elevator than Adam froze. He looked around and down the hallway, seeing many doors, which he counted. He refused to take a step forward.

What did he see?

What did he hear?

What did he smell?

I am impotent when it comes to imagining the multiple sensations and stimuli that overwhelm Adam in his miswired world of autism. His reaction? He would not move. I picked him up to carry him down the hallway to suite 201, but he became rigid. Like an animal smelling danger, he knew that where we were about to go was not safe.

Four months of waiting for this appointment. We were going in. Or so I thought.

Jumping out of my arms and magnetizing himself to the floor, I left him flailing as I ran down the hallway to let the office staff know that we were outside, but it was going to take some effort to get Adam through the door. The distance of the hall to the office door grew farther and farther as I parted from Adam, now screaming on the floor outside the elevator. I had never left Adam alone before, not even for six steps. Patricia, the office manager, calmly came out, by which time I was already back on the floor trying to pick Adam up. She let me know not to worry, "We see this all the time," which is why they cleverly schedule patients like Adam an hour before the actual appointment. Regardless, we did not make it into the office that day.

Patricia rescheduled us for another appointment, this time only two months out, and she suggested that we start making weekly visits to the office, to at least get through the door, maybe into an exam room, maybe even seated in a dental chair, before the day of the now-rescheduled dental exam. And so, we began. Week after week we drove to Dr. Lovenger's office in Mission Viejo, and week after week, Adam began to react farther and farther away from our destination. By the fourth week, all we did was get on the 5 Freeway going south when he started to cry; he did not have the words yet, but his crying "*No crocodile*" meant "*No dentist.*" It was no small feat to decode this and make the connection—oh! The Shel Silverstein poem:

The Crocodile's Toothache

The Crocodile
Went to the dentist
And sat down in the chair,
And the dentist said, "Now tell me, sir,
Why does it hurt and where?"
And the Crocodile said, "I'll tell you the truth,
I have a terrible ache in my tooth,"
And he opened his jaws so wide, so wide,
The the dentist, he climbed right inside,
And the dentist laughed, "Oh isn't this fun?"
As he pulled the teeth out, one by one.
And the Crocodile cried, "You're hurting me so!
Please put down your pliers and let me go."
But the dentist laughed with a Ho Ho Ho,
And he said, "I still have twelve to go-
Oops, that's the wrong one, I confess,
But what's one crocodile's tooth more or less?"
Then suddenly, the jaws went SNAP,
And the dentist was gone, right off the map,
And where he went one could only guess...
To North or South or East or West...
He left no forwarding address.
But what's one dentist, more or less?

-Shel Silverstein

Source credit: https://www.google.com/search?q=the+crocodile+and+the+dentist&source=lnms&tbm=isch&sa=X&ved=0ahUKEwi9hMCNu6rUAhVDjVQKHSMtD_4Q_AUICygC&biw=1247&bih=611#tbm=isch&q=the+crocodile's+toothache&imgrc=kSWMGUP_sILvQM

Indeed, I was getting better and better at speaking "Adam."

Of course, I became more stridently determined that Adam *had* to see Dr. Lovenger, if only to earn my merit badge for "excellence in parenting" yet it is tough to know how far to push or when, as Han Solo advised in *Star Wars*: "let the Wookie win."

Patricia then recommended that our best next step would be to schedule an outpatient exam at the local hospital, which would allow Adam to be under full sedation while Dr. Lovenger worked on his teeth. And thus, the coordinating of benefits began.

The first hurdle was convincing our dental insurance company that Adam required this level of care for his dental procedures. It took numerous appeals to Delta Dental to convince them that Adam needed to be sedated prior to dental treatment—"Yes, even for the initial exam." We next jumped into our medical benefits and worked with Blue Shield to pay for the outpatient "surgery" where the exam and any subsequent treatment would be performed. With Patricia's help, it still took seven months to coordinate the benefits and agreements of who would pay for what. So doing the math, it took us eleven months to finalize the plan for Adam to have his teeth checked and cleaned. Patience—that is all it takes, as if patience is an easy attribute to acquire.

Having learned from my past mistakes, Adam and I began our "field trips" to St. Joseph's outpatient pavilion weeks in advance to help him acclimate to yet another new place. I talked him through each step and prior to the actual morning, we had accomplished four successful visits. Because the operating rooms were behind many closed doors, and the waiting area was sunlit with colorful pictures on the walls, it was not as scary as the dark hall of an office building. I tried to imagine what it felt like through Adam's hyper-sensitive sensory system.

I feared that somewhere back in Adam's memory, he recalled our very first visit to CHOC when he had that first ABR and that he knew exactly what we were going into—despite my best efforts to hide the truth from him. We took our last "field trip" to St. Josephs the afternoon before the appointment, took care of all the preadmission work and hoped all would go well the next morning.

Ha! We plan, and God laughs. I was wrong again. Any deviation in Adam's routine causes him stress. He was not allowed to eat from 6:30 p.m. the night before—so starting the day without having his morning waffle upset him. Not putting on his backpack and waiting for the bus at 7:40 a.m. upset him. Having to get in the car and drive north on the 5 Freeway upset him. And any hopes of getting my merit badge for "excellence in parenting" would not stand up in a court of law when it was exposed that (upon doctor's orders) I slipped him a Valium cocktail to reduce this anticipated stress. Hence, despite his initial confusion, Adam was one mellow guy by the time we got to St. Joseph's outpatient pavilion. I wish I could say the same for myself.

Lumbering peacefully in my arms, we were greeted by Dr. Lovenger's staff who had five outpatients scheduled for that morning. I had not realized that part of the reason that it took so long was that they were coordinating several patients who required this level of care.

Go figure. We are not the only family on the planet with special needs.

Patricia invited me back into the preparation room where I was given my own hospital greens to put on. To my surprise, I was invited to be part of the Adam's team. Thanks to the Valium cocktail, Adam did not resist being undressed and having the blue-and-white hospital gown put on him. "Apron?" he asked. I did not know he knew that word.

"Apron," I replied.

It was okay not to have a language lesson at this moment.

Sheryl, Dr. Lovenger's dental assistant, with whom I had also worked for weeks in getting this day coordinated, was surprised to see me back there.

"Do you think this is a good idea?" I heard her whisper to Dr. Lovenger.

"Excellent idea," interjected Dr. Peck, Adam's anesthesiologist to whom I had just been introduced.

I did exactly as I was told. Dr. Lovenger handed me a paper cup with another Valium cocktail in it. "For me?" I asked hopefully.

Dr. Lovenger laughed as a nurse covered my face with a surgical mask and put white latex gloves on my hands.

"Give it to Adam," he said with a wink. "We are pleased you are in here with us, Sheila."

I felt like Roy Neary being invited onto the mother ship at the end of *Close Encounters of the Third Kind.* "I wish more parents could help us in this way."

And then Dr. Lovenger sighed. "I wish I could help all the Adams in the world."

They had me carry Adam down the hall into the surgical room where Dr. Peck was already waiting for us, sitting amid an array of medical breathing circuits and anesthetic devices—vaporizers, ventilators, and pressure gauges. All this preparation for what the rest of the world, and even a crocodile, are able to do as we sit quietly in a dental chair. Nope, being autistic is not for sissies.

"Will you be here the entire time?" I asked Dr. Peck.

"Yep, and most importantly, I will be here when Adam wakes up."

Dr. Peck covered Adam's little face with the breathing mask. "Here we go," said Dr. Lovenger.

For them, it was just another day. Routine. All in a day's work.

X-rays.

Exam.

Six cavities.

Drilling.

Fillings.

Sealant on the rest of the teeth.

Cleaning.

Just no "spit."

For me, a whole new experience. I felt relief as Adam slept peacefully on the gurney, tubes in his nose, in this deepened, unconscious state of being. I wondered if he really had to be put under. I wondered if he felt as peaceful as he looked lying there without distress. I wondered if he felt some relief in not having to fight against the sensations that perpetually jump out at him and interrupt his world—just for this little bit of time.

I wondered why Dr. Lovenger had invited me back there.

Was it for them?

For Adam?

For me? It was not the first time that I doubted my usefulness.

There was nothing for me to do. But it did not matter; I was grateful to be part of the team.

The procedures over, Dr. Lovenger and his team were ready to move onto his next patient already prepped and waiting in another room. A second gurney was rolled into postop and linked to the first one so that I could crawl onto the bed and be right next to Adam as he reemerged into the world.

It was a peaceful, calm awakening.

Dr. Lovenger came in to check on us.

"Thank you," I said. "Thank you for helping my Adams in the world."

"See you in three years."

"I'll start coordinating the benefits now!"

Dr. Lovenger laughed.

Not sure why he thought I was kidding.

Years later, I was asked to write a piece for a compilation of short plays on tolerance and acceptance. *Cootie Shots: Theatrical Inoculations Against Prejudice and Bigotry* was the brainchild of two creative and daring theater artists whose vision was to compile a play for children that addressed social issues. Kind of like Marlo Thomas's *Free to Be You and Me* but for the new millennium of children. (http://www.cootie-shots.org/cootie.html). It was to be a piece about being a kid with special needs. Of course, it was about my son, and I knew immediately what its title would be: "All the Adams in the World."

Thank you, Dr. Lovenger.

Excerpted from *Cootie Shots: Theatrical Inoculations
Against Bigotry for Kids, Parents and Teachers*
A Fringe Benefits Book, Copyright 2001
Theater Communications Group Inc.

*Kid # 1 and Kid #2 are young teens. ADAM and INNER ADAM
(Adam's feelings and thoughts that he can't express) also young teens, are
dressed in the same clothes.*

KID #1	Funny!
KID #2	Weird!
KID #1	Why does he do that?
INNER ADAM	Don't stare at me!
KID #1	But he's so…
KID #2	He's so…
KID #1 and KID #2	He's so…
KID #2	Funny!
KID #1	Weird!
KID #2	Why doesn't he talk?
INNER ADAM	I talk… I REALLY talk—
ADAM	*Green Eggs and Ham!*
KID #1 and KID #2 (annoyed)	*Green Eggs and Ham?*
ADAM (building)	*Casey Junior!*
KID #1 and KID #2 (taunting)	Casey Junior!
ADAM (angrily)	*The Wonderful Wizard of Oz!*
KID #1 *(directed sardonically at Adam)*	What is his problem?

(Adam puts his index finger in his mouth and hits his head with the fist of his other hand. He is frustrated and makes an angry sound. There is no doubt that he especially upset and angry.)

KID #2   Oh…My…God…
                               What…A…Psycho

(KID #1 and KID #2 give ADAM looks of total disgust and disbelief)

INNER ADAM (to ADAM)   Stop it! Stop it! You're twelve years
                               old!
                               Look at the way they're looking at
                               us! Why do you keep embarrass-
                               ing us?!

ADAM   Kermit the Frog! (pause)
                               Tarzan!

INNER ADAM (shift in tone)   Precious, you're so precious, I'm so
                               precious, But they can't see it.
ADAM   I want Chuckie Cheese—eight
                               pizzas—YES!

(KID #1 and KID #2 point and laugh)

INNER ADAM   Stop staring at me! Stop Staring at
                               me! Can't you see I want to fit in?
                               I want to play and be your friend.
                               But all I can say is:
ADAM   *Jiminy Cricket!*
INNER ADAM   Or
ADAM   *The Jungle Book!*
INNER ADAM   It's all in my head and my heart—
                               I'm just a kid who came out
                               miswired!

KID #1	What a freak!
KID #2	(whispering conspiratorially) I hear he's artistic
INNER ADAM	Autistic! Autistic! And it's not my fault! Please do not look at me that way!
ADAM (singing)	Zippidy doo dah—Zippidy ay! My-oh-my what a wonderful day!
INNER ADAM	Autistic—I'm really a genius but I'm all locked up…inside of me! My language is all that I hear, memorized inside of me! But when you hear—
ADAM (autistic voice)	Kermit the Frog!
INNER ADAM	What I am really saying is:
ADAM (in a regular, warm and compassionate voice)	"It's not easy being green!"
INNER ADAM	It's so hard to be different, to not fit in, to be like a frog, judged by your appearance, and when you hear—
ADAM (autistic voice)	The Jungle Book!
INNER ADAM	What I am telling you is to:
ADAM (in a fun and vivacious singing voice)	Look for the bare necessities
	The simple bare necessities Forget about your worries and your strife!
INNER ADAM	And even when you hear:
ADAM (autistic voice)	TARZAN!
INNER ADAM	I'm telling you that "You'll be in my heart"
ADAM (singing)	"Yes, you'll ne in my heart"

INNER ADAM	Don't you get it? I'm reaching out to you—trying to connect—in the only way I know how. But it all makes sense to me.
KID #1	What's autistic?
KID #2	My mom says he's in a world of his own.
	She doesn't know how his parents can love him.
	She thinks they should put him in an institution and get on with their lives.
KID #1	Funny!
KID#2	Weird!
KID #1	Why does he do that?
INNER ADAM	If only they could listen
KID #1	But he's so…
KID #2	He's so…
KID #1 and KID #2	He's so…

(KID #1 and KID #2 exit together)

ADAM *(singing)*	When you wish upon a star
	Makes no difference who you are
	When you wish upon a star
	Your dreams come true…
INNER ADAM	(loving puts arm around ADAM)
	Jiminy Cricket!

Postscript:

It was a Saturday night in April 2000 when we attended a preview performance of *Cootie Shots* being performed by the original Fringe Benefits cast prior to their first tour. The show didn't start until 8:00 p.m., which was past Adam's bedtime, so we were not surprised that he was tired and restless, twitching and making his noises. People in the audience were becoming annoyed with us, staring us down with "The Look," secretly wishing we would take Adam and leave. And then they got to "All the Adams in the World." When the actor playing Adam said, "Kermit the Frog," Adam's level of attention completely shifted. When the actor playing Adam shouted "Eight pizzas—yes!" a look of horror came across Adam's face. He knew this was about him. No, not about him—this *was* his life, his world on stage. I cringed with deep remorse as I realized that I had not only written a play about my son, but I was allowing his life to be put on stage without having asked his permission to do so. How could I have been so thoughtless, clueless, heartless? I did not know how to apologize for this betrayal of his trust.

And then, the lady in the row behind us realized something even more profoundly—the boy she had been directing those looks of disgust toward for the past fifteen minutes was *that* boy in the play who was being laughed at by *those* kids. A wave of understanding flooded across the audience, as one by one, people began to realize the connection of themselves to the play they were watching. And everyone had looks of sadness and remorse as they realized that the roles they had been playing were the same as Kid 1 and Kid 2.

Funny.

Weird.

Art imitating life.

Life imitating art.

There was no applause when Adam and Inner Adam left the stage.

Shame and embarrassment filled the audience. Not the impact anyone anticipated.

Of course, it was Adam who broke the tension: "Jiminy Cricket."

CHAPTER 9

He Got His Wings

As "normies," we take a multitude of things—if not everything—for granted. We learn by watching, touching, tasting, feeling, listening to our mommies and daddies when they assure us that "everything is going to be okay."

But what if your world is constantly overwhelmed by those senses which have been designed to help you navigate the world? What if language is but gobbledygook and Mommy's hugs make your body wrack with discomfort? And what if the way you understand and interpret the world is through the movies and cartoons you watch over and over and over again because the images on the screen make more sense to you than the people who are trying to bring you into their world because they have no way of coming into yours?

Oh, if only I had had this wisdom as I tried to force Adam into every opportunity that we provided for Josh. School, soccer, movies, theater, playdates, baseball, dentist, roller skating, riding a bike, swimming, dances, and above all, summer camp. Now, I was not completely ridiculous in the ways I sought out these opportunities.

I knew that if I wanted Adam to play soccer, that I would have to lead the charge to create the AYSO VIP Program in our region. For us to survive a day at Disneyland, we would have to get that special-needs front-of-line pass (back in the days when it was a *shhhhh…* secret), amid the scornful comments that we were "going in the exit, ma'am." But residential summer camp—not so easy. Of course, there was Easter Seals and the Jay Nolan Camps, but because we, as a family, grew up with the Jewish Residential Camp experience, I was committed that Adam, like Josh, like their dad, like me, would have this same opportunity.

Enter Camp Kutz in Warwick, New York.

Yes, Warwick, New York, had a special ten-day program for Jewish children, ages nine to sixteen, with autism. I learned about the camp in February 1997, and thus my mission began—Adam would go to Camp Kutz in July.

Now, I could digress and spend the rest of this chapter talking about living in the reality of Adam's needs (rather than mine) and looking for summer camps closer to home—after all, Easter Seals had been sponsoring camps since the 1950s, but I did not *want* Adam to be singing "This Little Light of Mine" and pledging himself during the Christian Rag Ceremony (as if he would keep a scarf tied around his neck). I wanted him to have the same experiences as Josh—Jewish art, dancing, songs, prayer, and Shabbat. I dreamed about singing Debbie Friedman and Julie Silver songs with my boy as we danced with Miriam's timbrels.

I will also forego writing about my pit bull tenacity in contacting Camp Kutz, months of conversations with the director of the Kesher (Connections) Program and my lobbying for Adam to be accepted, because I, despite my determination, try to be a reasonable person, and I understood the restrictions—that the session was limited to ten campers with autism, that the Camp Kesher Director, Kim, was not only selecting individual campers, but she was putting together a group of children who would be able to live together for the ten days and who would be good matches for the counseling staff. I understood all that. Yet, I was relentless in my convictions and enthusiasm for Adam to go to Jewish summer camp because Josh had his first experience at summer camp when he was nine years old—and Adam would *not* miss out! Back in 1997, as I was fiercely advocating for what I deemed was best and most important for Adam, I had forgotten the lesson from Steven J and his mom, for I had forgotten to ask, "Does Adam want to go to summer camp? Does he have any concept of what summer camp is?" I showed him pictures of the camp activities.

"Adam, do you want to go in the canoe?"

"Canoe, yes!"

"Honey, look at the art barn. Do you want to do art?"

"Art barn, yes!"

"Sweetie, do you know what this is? It is a campfire!"

"Fire. Dragon. Yes!"

I did not take the time to ponder if ten days and nights *might* be too long a period for Adam's first time away from home. Perhaps, one or two nights in a bed other than his own would be more appropriate. Nope, not me. I did not even consider that Adam would not be accepted. I had him snuggled tightly in a sleeping bag as we practiced camping out in the back yard. We went to the beach on Saturday nights to sit around the campfire. I introduced him to s'mores and hot dogs and increased swimming lessons to three times a week. We even went to Disneyland numerous times (because the SoCal pass was only $180.00 a year back then) to paddle the canoes around Tom Sawyer's Island. We were ready! But then, there was this one thing—a critically important factor—that I had failed to consider. *How* were we going to get Adam to New York?

There is so much in our adult, experienced world that we take for granted—a thousand different moments that we hardly recognize when we go out into the world. Even with our nonautistic children, we simply pack them up and go and assume that they will easily adapt to whatever new situation is put before them. Such is not the case in the lives of people with autism. Structure and routine are necessary for them to make sense of their lives. Once again, this is a lesson that I learned and forgot, learned and forgot, learned and forgot.

A couple of weeks before we were to leave for New York, it occurred to me that taking a "short airplane" trip as a precursor to the longer trip to Newark would be a good idea, and so, I bought us tickets to fly to San Francisco and back. It would be a forty-five-minute flight—we would fly up—have lunch at the airport and then fly home. Easy-peasy. Remember, in 1997, we were all allowed into the boarding area, where we still had the joy of watching arrivals and departures, so full of human emotion. Adam and I packed up for the journey, drove to John Wayne Airport, full of excitement for the adventure! Or at least, that was how I was reading the situation.

The first challenge was getting through security screening; what I learned here was that Adam did not want to put his backpack through the security scanner; in fact, he refused to take it off. Then, I was not allowed to walk with Adam through the full-body scanner, which he was incapable of walking through without touching the sides. So then, airport security, pre-TSA, isolated Adam from me to wave the magic want over his body—another stressor as his backpack lay on the conveyor out of his reach. "The Looks" began as Adam began to cry "backpack, backpack."

And because I was in my "I am Mom, hear me roar" mode, I had not considered to invite anyone to go with us to help me out at the airport. It never occurred to me (back then) to admit that I might need some help. Nope, not me.

The time finally came to board our flight. I had arranged for early boarding. The gate attendant took our tickets and tore them, and as we approached the jetway, Adam froze. He looked ahead, looked at me, looked ahead and then screamed, "No!" He threw himself onto the ground becoming a speed bump over which no one else could pass. If you have never seen a child in an autistic meltdown, imagine that this person's body becomes completely rigid, immovable, as if magnetized to the earth, screaming the pain of a wounded animal. And because he speaks in "Adam talk," his yelps of "No Wizard of Oz, no Wizard of Oz" made no sense to me.

The stares burned holes in us.

"Ma'am," the attendant at the gate began, "is your son going to get on the plane?"

"Ma'am, you have to move your son so that other passengers can board."

"Ma'am, we have a schedule to follow."

Pause, pause, pause.

"Ma'am! Is your son going to get on the plane or not?"

I was on the floor with Adam, trying to calm him, trying to explain, trying to lift him off the ground. He began to flail, arched his back, and screamed even louder, "No Wizard of Oz!"

Security arrived. It took three men to lift him off the ground. His arms swinging, his legs kicking, I grabbed his backpack and we were moved out of the way. I stumbled, holding back my own terror or feelings of failure or shame or embarrassment or fear or anger or *only God knows* what I was feeling, for all I could think was, "I have to help my son." We were glared at, stared at: looks of horror and disgust, looks of pity and helplessness. An older man said, "People like that should not be allowed on planes." A younger woman and her husband picked up their own children in fear. A woman approached. "I am a nurse, can I help?"

"Please, don't miss your flight," I implored. The last thing I needed was for someone to be nice to us.

My head swirled; my heart raced; I wanted to throw up; I wanted to hide; but all I did was get back down on the floor with Adam, far away from the gate and rock him until he was calmed so we could leave. I had no idea how much time has elapsed. I looked up to see that the doors to the jetway had been closed, and as I looked out the glass windows onto the runway, the plane began to slowly back away from the gate with two empty seats that should have been occupied by Adam and me.

When we got home, I got Adam settled in front of the TV, and I began moving furniture—rearranging the family room and moving all the bookcases, because that was my best coping strategy. I thought and thought and thought, Pooh Bear, "Think, think, think."

How are we going to get Adam to New York?

Someone must know someone who knew someone who knew someone who could help us.

There are many things I am not, but one thing I am is a problem solver.

We needed to practice—we needed to practice!

And that is how we met an angel on earth—because someone knew someone who knew someone who knew someone who was willing to help us.

- Valerie was my neighbor who lived across the street.
- Valerie was a waitress who worked with Jane.
- Jane's stepfather ran the ground crew at John Wayne Airport.
- Jane's stepfather was friends with Jan, who worked for Northwest Airline.
- Jan oversaw boarding at gate 3 at John Wayne Airport.
- Jan called me and set up a plan to help Adam learn how to board an airplane.

Oh, the things we do that we take for granted. Oh! The connecting web to helping my son.

Jan oversaw a flight every morning at 7:00 a.m.—the first one out the gate each day.

Jan had us meet her at gate 3 the next Monday morning at 6:30 a.m., and for the next two weeks, Monday through Friday,

(Photo credit: https://acidemic. blogspot.com/2010/07/great-acid-cinema-wizard-of-oz-1939.html)

Jan worked with us, helping us to get Adam down the jetway to the plane.

Days 1, 2, and 3—Adam was tightly swaddled in his Winnie the Pooh blanket, as we approached the jetway. "No Wizard of Oz!"

It took me a few days to decode his message, and then it hit me; if you remember your Wizard of Oz trivia, Dorothy, the Tin Man, the Scarecrow and the Lion had to walk down a cavernous hallway, that looked very much like the jet-way that loomed before us, and at the end of that hallway was a door that opened to the very frightening face of the Great and Powerful Oz.

Of course, Adam was afraid of what lie ahead.

Slowly he walked—step by step, inch by inch—so that by Friday, we had made it to the entrance of the plane. Once again, paralyzed with fear, Adam stopped, grounded himself, and refused to take that one last step over the thresh hold.

His dad had had enough. He picked Adam up, holding him close.

"No Wizard of Oz," he calmly assured our son. "No Wizard of Oz."

Then *splat!* Like Wilde E. Coyote sprawled against a desert wall before being hit on the head by an Acme anvil, Adam had all fours glued to the entrance of the jet. Arm and leg, leg and arm, we peeled him off the siding and carried him onto the plane.

And then—Silence. Bewilderment. Calm.

Adam stood at the front of the plane, eyeing first class (as if *that* was going to happen!), sliding out of his father's arms. He stood there, me blocking the exit of the plane, his dad bracing for what might happen next.

And Adam said, "Bus."

Bus—yes! It's like a flying bus!

And we were on.

"No Wizard of Oz."

The next week we practiced walking down the jetway, practiced holding a ticket, saw the cockpit, and put a suitcase in the overhead storage bin. We even explored the bathrooms and assured Adam that he would be safe—even if he had to pee!

On the last day, Angel Jan had a breakfast ordered and delivered so that Adam could practice eating on an airplane. We were ready!

How can we ever thank this woman, who ran gate 3, who knew the man who ran the ground crew, whose stepdaughter was a waitress, who worked with Val, who lived across the street from me?

Angel Jan gave Adam his wings.

And he had an incredible experience at Camp Kutz, where he went every summer for the next seven years.

For the full story please go to https://www.latimes.com/archives/la-xpm-1997-jul-29-me-17248-story.html

CHAPTER 10

Shall We Dance?

Oh, junior high school. I shudder with the memories of those days. I was in junior high during deeply turbulent years full of political upheaval, controversy, and life-changing, historical events that are forever imprinted on my heart. Martin Luther King and Bobby Kennedy were both assassinated. The Vietnam War and Woodstock. Richard Nixon was elected president. Neal Armstrong walked on the moon. And it goes without saying that nothing affected our world more than the day it was announced that the Beatles broke up. Nearly twenty years later when *The Wonder Years* aired, I watched each week as each episode retold the story of my own days at Ball Junior High School in Anaheim, California. Heck, my brother even had a garage band. These are the memories that all of us baby boomers share, those of us who were in junior high school in the late sixties.

It is only in retrospect that I appreciate the significant impact of those years because like most adolescents, I had the maturity of an out-of-control thirteen-year-old who was caught up in the drama of junior high.

Who would be cheerleader?

Would our football team beat our cross-town rival?

Was my dress shorter than the allowed "two inches above the knee" rule (yes, the vice principal, Mr. Jenkins, would have us kneel to the ground before him as he measured the distance between the bottom of our hem to the ground with his ruler).

And the horrors of dressing out for PE—first because we had to shower publicly and even worse, where our fat, and I do mean fat, gym teacher would have us stand before her so she could take inventory on the shape of our legs. "I am looking for your 'three peepholes, ladies," the physical standard of beauty which she convinced us was necessary if we ever wanted to become a model. Twiggy was the icon of the day with her Bambi eyes, thin lips, and tiny frame. They did not call her Twiggy for nothing. And here I stood with big lips, big hips, wearing glasses and braces. It was possible to see daylight through the empty space between my ankles and calves, but my thighs were far too thick to have the third mandatory peephole; alas, girls whose grandparents immigrated from Poland at the turn of the century were of peasant stock; we were built to pick potatoes and bear children. A third peephole I had not, and so Mrs. Elmgreen declared, "No modeling career for you!" Me being a model was highly doubtful, peepholes or not, for I stood a mere 4'11" and was thirty pounds overweight, even in junior high. There is not a time I do not remember being on a diet—but that is fodder for another book.

And so, as the Beach Boys sang about every other *California Girl* at Ball Junior High, all of whom looked so cool with their silky blond hair and bell bottoms and who could boast of having three peepholes in their legs, I was the lonely bagel on the plate of lovely croissants. Which is why of all the traumatizing events during my personal *Wonder Years*, nothing was as devastating as the after-school dances, otherwise known as sock hops.

On the last Friday of every month, we had an after-school sock hop. The cafetorium was turned into the dance hall, lights dimmed, music blaring, shoes piled along the back and side walls and stinky feet, stinky armpits, all the stinky smells of four hundred kids in puberty trying our best to be as cool as the older high school kids we religiously watched on *Shebang* and *9th Street West* from whom we thought we learned how to dance. There were special dances too— the yearly seventh-, eighth-, and ninth-grade dances, the Halloween Costume Dance, the Valentine's Dance, and even the United Way Fund-Raiser Dance, where I would go with the hopes of maybe, tonight, one boy will ask me to dance. But no, I stood on the side-lines with all the other invisible undesirables, watching with envy as I dreamed of being out there on the dance floor. I would longingly gaze at the dance floor while the pretty, popular girls, whose hips and hair swayed (or jerked) to the music were repeatedly asked to dance. This was before the days when, unlike today, girls had fig-ured out that it was much more fun to take over the dance floor in large groups. It was before *Roe v. Wade*; we did not know we had any rights. And when Janis Ian came out with her song "At Seventeen." I cried myself to sleep once a month on Friday nights listening to *that* song, knowing that this was as good as it was ever going to get.

So is it any wonder that I was filled with severe anxiety when it came time for Adam to transition into (what they now call) mid-dle school? He turned eleven during the summer of 1998. Middle school was now for sixth, seventh, and eighth graders, and Adam had reached the age for sixth; there was nothing I could do to slow down his childhood. Autistic or not, he was entering adolescence. He would still be part of the OCDE Special Education Program, but would now attend classes at a local middle school. Most of his school day would be spent in his special world with the amazing team from OCDE, but because socially he had made noticeable progress in relating to others, it was recommended that he be mainstreamed into a couple of classes with *all* the other kids on campus.

Deep breath. Deep breath.

The good news was that Adam had reached a level of interac-tion where the IEP team felt that (with support) he could successfully interact with his typical peers. A number of kids from the elementary school knew him and because the county program had been housed at Rancho for six years, there were members of the staff who had learned to welcome our special kids into their classes.

Which classes? PE and art. Maybe music. "We'll see how it goes."

Art would be a great choice; the tactile, kinesthetic projects would fall under the category of "occupational therapy" special edu-cation language.

But PE? Adam would have to "dress out" changing into the required black shorts and white shirt. He would have no difficulties with this, and I had no concerns about him memorizing his lock combination. If given the numbers, he could memorize the combinations for every boy in the locker room. It was the memories of sitting on the black top, gritty rocks working their way into my underpants while the best athletes, the team captains, would pick "her—him—her—him," pointing a powerful index finger at the next member of their team that concerned me. The memory was too close to the rejection of waiting to be asked to dance at a sock hop. Who would pick Adam for their team? Not that Adam would care. He wouldn't. He would happily sit on "his number" and wait to be picked. It would not matter to him whether that fickle finger of fate selected him or not. As long as the PE teacher allowed him to stand/sit on the same number painted on the black top for roll call, he should be fine. "Please—don't change his number, Coach!" But then, after class, whether he worked up a sweat or not, he would have to take a shower. Yes, his body was changing, and like all disgusting adolescent boys, Adam could get stinky. Very stinky. Getting him to wear deodorant had its challenges. But a shower—a public shower? Where kids could tease him or hide his underwear? And once he got into the shower, would he ever get out? Adam loved showers. He might just enjoy standing under the warm water longer than he should. Because after all, in middle school, the bell rings and like Pavlov's dog, the kids must run to their next class within five minutes. Truth be told, I had the same worries the year before when Josh "graduated" to middle school. If Josh were ever attacked by the bullies, he would easily be able to fend them off...or so I wanted to believe. But Adam? Adam? Who knew? Well, I had already been trusting the county program for the past six years. I knew that they knew better than me. Reluctantly, I followed their lead. "We'll see how it goes."

Getting Adam ready to make the transition to middle school was an important step for which the county program was fully prepared. Starting in May, Adam would go over to Rancho a couple of times a week to meet his new teacher and the students, most of whom he knew from when he was with them in the preschool and elementary years. "Rashad—March 12, 1985. Brian—August 2, 1986. Sara—May 9, 1987." Adam knew them all—and their birthdays—and how old they would be in the year 2312. He was great with numbers. He learned the campus, got to practice changing clothes for PE, and even took a shower a couple of times. As predicted, he did not want to get out. I said a special prayer for the PE teacher who ignored our advice and foolishly gave Adam a different number to stand on for roll call come next September. My boy liked routine—permanent routine. By the end of July, after his elementary school graduation, Adam was as prepared as he could be to enter middle school. All the bases had been covered. "Bye-bye, Meadowpark."

It was the last week of August when all the registration papers arrived for Middle School Round Up. Because Adam would officially be enrolled in two classes outside of the county program, we needed to fill out additional paperwork for the local school district. In the packet were familiar forms, the same ones that I had filled out for Josh every year, so nothing was surprising: health forms, PTA, library card, supplemental insurance, etc. Also included was the paperwork for school pictures, ASB, field trip permission slips, and the yearly dance pass for the same sock hops and sixth-, seventh-, eighth-grade dances that were still a traditional part of those formative years. Except in Adam's packet, the checkmark for the dance pass had been crossed off in black sharpie. A big, fat, indelible black line that in my mind read: "Your son is *not* welcome at the dances."

I was incensed, infuriated, spitting mad with anger. "Adam has every right to attend those dances," I ranted. "How dare they? It is my decision as the parent if Adam attends dances, not the district. Damn District. Still stacking the deck."

The packet arrived in Saturday's mail, which gave me two days to plan how I was going to tear into whomever it was that used that black sharpie to cross off "dance pass." The nerve. The intolerance. What a disgrace. Hadn't over two hundred thousand people gathered on August 28, 1963, with MLK in Washington, DC, for a political rally known as the March on Washington for civil rights and freedom and the right to attend middle school dances? Didn't Congress pass the Americans with Disabilities Act (ADA) in 1990, the comprehensive civil rights law addressing the needs of people with disabilities? The ADA prohibits discrimination in employment, public services, public accommodations, telecommunications, *and* middle school dances. Oh! I was primed for a fight. No one puts Adam in the corner!

The first thing Monday morning I was on the phone with Adam's principal. We had worked closely with Dr. Walker since Adam entered the county program, and I was thrilled that she had just been given the added responsibility of overseeing the middle school program. I had no doubts that she would be next to me on the warpath as together we stormed the special education office for the district program. "Drea, I need to meet with you. *Today*." She had me come in at two o'clock that afternoon.

This was not the first time Andrea Walker had to talk me off a ledge. She had been our tour guide during that first visit to the county program back in February 1991. She helped us strategize when yet another new Director of Special Education for district insisted that they could *now* independently meet the needs of our moderate to severe students and planned to cancel its contract with the county program. We all knew it was only about balancing the budget during the years of Orange County's bankruptcy. Dr. Walker was always looking for ways to fund enrichment programs so that our kids could go with every other second grader to the Pacific Symphony or see a play with the fourth graders. She was our champion, and I knew she would be on board to fight this violation of Adam's right to dance.

Dr. Walker listened to me rant. She wiped my tears. And she listened to me rant some more. She nodded in agreement that as his parent, I was the one to decide whether Adam should attend the dances. She could not have been more supportive in acknowledging that it had indeed been very wrong for someone to have crossed off the box for the dance pass with a big, fat, indelible black line. "So you'll come with me to the district office?" I implored.

"You know I support you," she replied with her amazing balance between professionalism and compassion, "but may I talk first?"

One thing I knew from my years of experience with Andrea Walker, was that even in my moments of embarrassing insanity, when I had no idea what I was talking about or when I would be asking for something that was completely unreasonable (although I hope that I did not behave that way too often) was that she would, foremost, respect me as a parent and, second, offer a voice of reason and perspective. Of course, she could talk, and of course, I would listen.

"So first off," she began, "I have a confession and I apologize. I made a mistake. The district sent the registration packet over to me and asked me to look it over before it was sent onto you. I was the one who instructed Lolly [the county secretary] to cross off dance pass. It was wrong of me, and I thank you for helping me to see that error. I am truly sorry."

How do you stay angry at an apology like that?

"But, Sheila, think about it. Middle school dances? The lights dimmed, the music blaring, shoes piled along the back and side walls and stinky feet, stinky armpits, all the stinky smells of four hundred kids in puberty? *Do you really think it would be good for Adam to be at those dances?*"

I took a deep breath and sighed a heavy sigh. She waited for me to reply. But I had nothing to say.

"Forgive me," she said once more, "but I have to ask you. What happened to you at your junior high dances that makes you want to use Adam to compensate for that hurt? Your son cannot undo whatever hurt you felt at those horrible dances."

My mouth snapped closed like a mousetrap catching its victim. She was right—100 percent right. I did not want Adam to feel the rejection and sadness that I felt at junior high dances. I wanted him to be included and popular; I had this vision that he could be dancing on the gym floor surrounded by kids who loved him and accepted him. I had forgotten the promise I had made to myself, the one I had learned from Mrs. J. I had failed to ask myself, "Whose need was I really meeting here?"

Swiss psychiatrist Elisabeth Kübler-Ross in her 1969 book, *On Death and Dying*, wrote about the five stages of grieving inspired by her work with terminally ill patients: denial, anger, bargaining, depression, and acceptance. As parents of children with severe disabilities, we experience these five stages repeatedly. We experience them every September when the five-year-olds in the neighborhood excitedly prepare for their first day of kindergarten, while our children have been riding the little yellow special education bus since they were three. We experience them when we show up for AYSO soccer and realize that the banner that displays "Everyone Plays" doesn't include our children. We experience them when we realize the lunacy of wanting our children to go to the middle school dances.

From that day on, I never went to an IEP or transition meeting for Adam without first checking in with myself: "Where am I on the emotional cycle of grieving my son's autism?" I should say, this could only happen *after* I gave myself permission to admit that Adam's dad was not the only parent living in denial, that I had been keeping myself overly consumed by autism to protect myself from the grief I felt for *what might have been*.

Sometimes I showed up wearing depression, and other times, it was anger. Before Adam's dad left us for his new life in Georgia, he came into an IEP with an agenda so complicated and long that it took three meetings and over twelve hours for us to realize that this was his way of dealing with his guilt for abandoning his son.

And at every milestone in Adam's life—when he entered high school, then college, then graduation and into the big, scary real world, I would revert back into denial, for I could not believe how fast our lives had flown.

I cycle through these emotions over and over and over again. Denial, anger, bargaining, depression, acceptance. It is no easy journey to get to *acceptance*, and once I get there, something else comes up that sends me back into earlier phases of the cycle. It's different than accepting a death, because for better or worse, life keeps coming at us.

We, the parents of children with severe disabilities, must learn to accept our children and love them for exactly who they are, not who we keep wishing they will become.

While other parents get to fret over which college their son will attend, I worry if Adam will make it through a day without hitting himself on the head or even worse, attacking his job coach. I agonize over what will happen to Adam when I am no longer on this planet. Birthday parties, sleepovers, driver's license, girlfriends, boyfriends, proms, graduations, marriage? These are dreams for other parents—not me.

The remarkable thing about Adam is that he has always been comfortable with himself; it's just that the rest of the world has not been so comfortable with him. If Adam had ever wanted any of these things, of course, I would fight to the bitter end to make them happen, but these have never been his needs, merely mine. At the risk of shaming myself even more with another embarrassing confession, I have to admit that I cannot state with full honesty that even after nearly thirty years, I have successfully embraced that last step—acceptance. I work on it every day. But I can promise you this, Adam is one of the (two) best things that has ever happened to me. I am so proud of him, and I thank God that I am the one who was chosen to be his mom.

My son, Adam, is the most *awe-tistic* person I know.

Addendum: In 2009, Adam "graduated" from his Transition Program at Orange Coast College. He was the valedictorian—mostly because he was the only one of the four graduates who could read! Nevertheless, I took great pride in this status. So we wrote his valedictory address in the mode that made the most sense to Adam— as a tribute to Dr. Seuss. Enjoy it here: https://www.youtube.com/watch?v=3eYSLGGeAbo&t=239s.

ADAM'S VALEDICTORIAN SPEECH— ORANGE COAST COLLEGE TRANSITION PROGRAM—JUNE 2009

Good Morning, Dear Teachers and Family and Friends,
Today our school journey has come to an end.
I loved school so much—every memory in file
So here is my speech—Adam alphabet style.
We've come here today to dance and to sing
For all of us who are graduating—
A is for **A**pplause for Amanda, Stephanie
And a round of **A**pplause for Mina and me!
B for Teacher Bob because he leads our team
He does all he can to make sure we succeed!
C is for Culverdale in preschool I began,
Here is the place where I started my plan!
D is for Dr. Seuss, who wrote my favorite stories
I can go right to his books every morning!
E is for education—that's why we are here,
Learning and growing so much every year!
F is for future—you all played a part,
We are **F**orever grateful in all of our hearts.
G is for **G**raduation—today is our day,
For Mina, Amanda, Stephanie and Adam—let's all
        say "Hooray!"
H is for Hillview—at this school I was happy,

Thank you, Teacher Patrick and Principal Abby!
I is for Irvine High School—Phillipe, Nancy were so
    good to me
And most special of all was our Teacher Dee!
Irvine was important to me, Oh my gosh!
I was there with my brother, yes **J** is for **J**osh!
K is for **K**athy O. who said "I can't wait to work with
    this special kiddo!"
The first of my teachers, she helped us to cope,
She has so much courage, she gave us such hope.
L is for **L**aidlaw who drove us each day,
To schools and back home, we were safe all the way!
M is for Meadowpark, Teachers Kim and **M**arie
I loved Teacher Pat and the **M**eadowpark Library.
N is for Northwest Airline, way up in the sky,
Jan Bernal gave me wings, she taught me to fly!
O-C-D-E—Drea, Howard and Bill—
O for **O**bama! I voted for him, and it was a thrill!
P—Be **P**repared! I sing loud and sing strong.
They are words I will use all my life long!
Q is for **Q**uestions that fill up my mind
"**Q**uiet Voice, Adam," I have heard a million times!
R is for Rancho—Junior High was first rate
Teacher Dawn was a wonder—she was also so great!
S is for Sharing O-C-D-E helped us stay calm
I am really going to miss my best, best friend, **S**aam
T is **T**ransition and **T** is for **T**ime,
T is the Class of 2009.
U—Understanding each **U**nusual day,
You **u**nlock the **U**niverse in so many ways.
V is for **v**ictory and teachers with style,
V is for **v**ery lucky and **v**ery special child.
W is for **W**ork Stations—Target and Trader Joes,
High Times and Lamp Post and Super Antojitos!
X—Extraordinary and **E**ven a savant,

But please, **e**xtra candy is what I really want!
Y is yourself—**you** should always be **you**,
So please remember 'To thine own self be true"
Z is for **z**esty—a shiny, bright jewel.
Zippidy Doo Dah—I've always loved school!
Thank for asking me to speak today
It's been such an honor on our special day
We are ready to graduate, we are ready to shine,
So **CONGRATULATIONS** to the class of 2009!

CHAPTER 11

Oh, Mandy!

Way back in the days of those Wednesday morning support group meetings at the ICEC, there were three women who never spoke about their children. It wasn't that they weren't involved—they were very much so. Rather, they were highly distracted by other events in their lives. When it was time for group sharing, it was without fail that one of these three women would start the session. The share always began at decibel level 10—or higher.

"That fucking asshole!"

All three of these mothers were engulfed in a horrific battle called *divorce*. These women were angry, so very, very angry, and week after week after week, they brought these emotions to our meetings. The details of their divorces were so complicated and painful that dealing with their child with special needs was easy in comparison.

The anger was not because of "the younger woman who that prick took off with," which two of the husbands did, nor was it because "that bastard accepted a new job in Minnesota and just packed up and left us," as did number three. The reason that all three of these women were enraged was because in each of their divorce settlements, the dads stipulated that they did not want to assume custodial responsibility for the child with the disability. Being a "no fault state" California law demanded that he pay child support for all children up to age eighteen, but there was no law demanding shared custody for a child with special needs. As I tried to imagine what they were going through, I would listen to their stories about maneuvering family court, the conflict between the parents, how the courts would divide the time between the parents, depending upon which parent better proved the other's inadequacies. But with these three, the circumstances of their divorces had been knocked sideways. These women were battling with the courts demanding that these fathers be required to share custodial responsibility for their child with special needs. Not only were these moms suffering the deep rejection of having been "dumped," the unkindest cut of all was that their disabled child was also being left behind. Damn right they were angry.

For the many challenges that we lived with, I counted my blessings that despite his denial of the diagnosis, Adam's dad loved our son and was actively involved in his life. We "tagged team" our way through many, many years—taking two cars wherever we went so that at least one of us could stay with Josh at family gatherings, the movies, soccer, or bowling, while the other left with Adam because he had just had too much. Who would stay and who would go most often depended upon which of us had the more patience on any given day in any given circumstance, and truthfully, Adam's dad usually won. He was a great dad, and it never occurred to me, despite my own beliefs that I was an unlovable person, that we would not be together as husband and wife and as a family of four. No one in my family had ever been divorced, and no one in his family had ever been divorced, or at least, no one ever talked about it, so that word, *divorce,* was just not part of our vocabulary. Or so I thought.

Whether it be proven fact or urban mythology, the divorce rate among parents of children with autism ranges between 64–80 percent, depending upon which report you read, or which talk show you watch. Expectations regarding the care and development of the child with autism (yes, the Ann Landers' article about thinking you are going to Italy but ending up in the Netherlands* is completely accurate when it comes to expectations), the never-ending pressures of handling the child's behaviors, juggling hectic schedules, financial challenges, battling with school districts and insurance companies and on and on and on, all contribute to extreme stress within the family. Yet another example about which Dr. Looney was right— evert aspect of our lives becomes affected. In the face of these challenges, and a national divorce rate of 40–50 percent, it's no wonder that marriages with children with autism result in even higher rates of divorce.

In 2001, we became part of the autistic statistic. I cannot say that the reason was due to the significant stresses and financial burdens that we experienced raising a child with autism. In fact, I believe that our commitment to Adam kept our marriage together long after it had run its course, and as Josh would later say, "Really, Mom, Dad left us long before he left us." He was completely accurate.

Just like I had observed so many years before at the ICEC, divorce is ugly. Like the women before me, it was a horrible divorce. Not surprisingly, like the men before him, Adam's dad was ready *not* to be a full-time dad. Initially, he stayed in our same city, but choosing to move to a one-bedroom apartment in a singles' community sent his message loud and clear: "I do not want joint custody and there is no room for our sons at my place."

Within a few months of his new life as a swinging single, I learned that Adam's dad had been actively searching the internet for a new wife.

The first time I heard her name, Mandy, was in the summer of 2003 just a few days before he would be flying to Atlanta, Georgia, to meet her for the first time. By April 2004, they had a private rendezvous in Vegas where they tied the knot, and on June 19 of the same year, less than twenty-four hours after Josh had received his high school diploma, Adam's dad had already packed up his entire life, loaded it into two pickup trucks and was driving into the sunset for his new life in the South. Mandy's mother and father were driving one of the trucks and Mandy was driving the other. The caravan looked like the frickin' Joads ready to embark across the great Dust Bowl. Joining them on this cross-country venture was Mandy's then eight-year-old son, her ten-year-old nephew, and Adam. I know— *what had I agreed to and why?*

How we got from a one-bedroom apartment in a singles' complex, where Adam could not spend the night, to Adam joining his dad and new stepmother on a three-thousand-mile cross-county journey to Atlanta is a story I never could imagine I would nor could nor should tell.

I credit both Mandy and me and our coming together as mothers, and *this* is the story I want to tell.

Mandy wanted to meet Adam.

On her turf.

It was with much trepidation that Adam's dad approached me about taking Adam to Atlanta with him for ten days over winter break, December 2003.

He asked me to meet him at a restaurant for lunch, without the boys.

I knew this must be something serious because the boys usually served as our buffer when we needed to speak. We both behaved better in front of our sons.

My first reaction when he told me he wanted to take Adam with him to meet Mandy was "*over my dead body*," and I got up and left the restaurant. It was a very short meeting.

There was no way I would let Adam out of my sight for ten days. Not with *him* and certainly not with *her*.

A few weeks passed, and Adam's dad asked me once again if I would meet with him.

"Are you going to ask me about taking Adam to Georgia?"

He wanted to tell me a few things about Mandy to "put my mind at ease."

He came over to the house, and he was different. He was speaking in a manner that was so unlike him, thanking me for all I had done for the boys over the past two years, and wouldn't it be good for me to have a break from the constant responsibilities of Adam? I did not buy it as far as I could throw it.

I have never learned to play chess and of my shortcomings, of which there are many, strategizing is not one of my better skills. Adam's dad is a master manipulator; he conquered the world numerous times when he played Risk, and I later learned that he was a more than proficient poker player, a fact he had kept hidden from me for many years. It was only in a momentary mistake by his only friend, Shannon, when he shared the rumor that Adam's dad met Mandy online in a poker game room; I say rumor because that is the story I was told. I really don't know for sure. So although I generally cannot see the next move on the game board of life, what I do know is dramatic literature, and it was so obvious to me that Mandy had scripted exactly what she wanted Adam's dad to say to me.

He told me of the "amazing coincidence in our lives" (me cringing when I realized that in his use of *our*, he was referring to another woman) that Mandy is a special education teacher with a specialty in autism and behavior disorders. He went on and on praising her for the awards she had received for her excellence in teaching and about the lives she had changed from her remarkable and successful strategies in the classroom. In fact, hadn't she already become a mentor to him as a teacher who was having more and more mainstreamed students placed in his second-grade class these days? How, during the summers, she had her own delivery business and how, being such an incredible mom, she would have her own son accompany her each day on her deliveries while she taught him how to multiply and spell and learn the state capitals. "She really is a wonderful person and teacher. It would be edifying for Adam to spend time with her." Are you kidding me? That man never uttered the word *edifying* in the twenty-three years I had known him; it was not in his vocabulary. Ah! That was the dead giveaway—Mandy had composed the script. And did I even hear him say *y'all* once or twice?

Truth be known, I was exhausted. And even though it scared me to let Adam go with his dad, maybe it wasn't such a bad idea for me to consider taking care of myself. Maybe. Sigh. Maybe. What, am I losing it completely? The thought that I would even consider considering this proposal made me sick to my stomach, and I am certain that my face had turned pea green. I did not trust him. I had no reason to trust him. This man had not said a kind word to or about me since 1999. He was incapable of being anything other than unkind, critical, cynical, and sarcastic. His need to provoke was insatiable. He derived pleasure from putting down people and in seeing people in emotional pain, most specifically me. So why the sudden change? What was this *about*?

It would never have occurred to me, honestly, not on any level, that within the next year, Adam's dad would have married Mandy and have moved to Atlanta, Georgia. It would have been completely implausible for me to even have tried to imagine this. If someone had told me he would be moving across the country, to the Deep South no less, three thousand miles away from his sons, I would never have believed it. The divorce was one thing, yet I always thought that was solely due to his contempt for me. But to move away from his sons? The only word I would come to associate with his choice was *abandon*. I would not know this was going to happen for six months more, and I promise you, on the day of this conversation, it had never entered my mind. Like I said, I do not anticipate the next move. But because we were in my home and the boys were there, albeit in different parts of the house, this time I could not just get up and walk away. I stopped for a moment to consider, "Could I allow Adam to go with his dad for ten days to meet Saint Mandy?"

I kept pondering those questions, *"Why the sudden change? What was this really about?"* Was it possible that he was returning to the person I once knew, the carefree man I met in 1980, the humorous, fun-loving lunatic, before he was burdened with work and marriage and children and autism? Although the words were clearly not his, had I seen a glimpse of the kind man I once knew and loved? Is it possible that his ugly midlife crisis was over? And what if Mandy really was all the things he said about her, especially that part—about wanting to meet Adam? No one had ever wanted to meet him before. So many people—both family and former friends—were afraid to know us anymore. I pondered this for several days, asking myself, "What am I so afraid of?" Even during our darkest days when their dad was so mean-spirited and cruel, he had never mistreated our boys. And it was with heartfelt tears when writing our divorce settlement that he acknowledged that it would be better for the boys to live with me. "Sheila is the stronger parent." On the other hand, there were things he did that were unforgivable, so why should I honor anything he wanted? He even tried to cut off child support for Josh when he turned eighteen, ignoring the clause that stated "either turning eighteen or high school graduation, whichever was the latter." Cheap bastard.

Back and forth, forth and back I went around and around in turmoil. It was my stubborn ego that refused to give it a chance. As much as there was a part of me that wanted to believe his sincerity, he had hurt me so deeply; he had been such an asshole. The question was selfish: "Why should he get what he wants when he had done so much damage?" And as I obsessed over and over on this, to the point of sleepless redundancy, ad nauseam, I realized that I had forgotten to ask the one question that I had learned to ask so long ago, "What is best for Adam?" I was so stuck in my own hurt, my own anger, my own story of being the abandoned wife with the disabled child, that I had once again failed to honor my son in the one thing I had promised. "How is this going to affect Adam?" I realized my hypocrisy, that just as I had sat in those parent support meetings eleven years prior judging those three moms for being so angry about their divorces that they forgot to focus on their kids, I was behaving no better. I knew what I was dealing with when it came to Adam's dad. There was only one thing I could do—call and introduce myself to Mandy.

"Are you crazy?" the women in my divorce recovery group gasped. "Why would you want to do that?" It is the right thing to do. I have lived with the conviction of putting aside my own anger, denial, sadness, disappointments, fears, and grief because none of that, none of that ever did anything to ever truly help my son. Here is the reality of the situation: for better or worse, I will always be connected to Adam's dad because he is the father of our children. He has never done anything to intentionally harm them. If I am truly ever going be able do what is best for Adam, I will have to be connected to him; perhaps meeting Mandy would be able to help us all. If my resentment blocks what is good for Adam, it is *not* good for Adam.

And the truth—the absolute, 100 percent undeniable truth—is that in all the years that we have had a son diagnosed with autism, this Mandy, this other woman who lives three thousand miles away, well, she is the first person who has ever reached out and said that she wants to meet Adam. And that means something—something I had never been told before.

Adam's dad wanted to know everything I was going to say to her before he agreed to give me her phone number. I could not tell him, not because I was being stubborn but because I honestly did not know. He was not happy with me, but I held my ground. I needed to know who this woman was before I could consider allowing Adam to go stay with her. That was the only way this was going to happen. I was nervous and uneasy to say the least. I made two promises to myself; one, I would not cry, and two, I would not say anything about the man whom she was cross-country dating. I figured that sooner or later, either she would figure him out or she wouldn't. So I put on my big-girl pants, my very most mature attitude, and most importantly, my "I am my son's advocate" hat, and I dialed her number. We had arranged the time, so she was expecting the call.

What *would* I say? What would I *say*? Her accent was as thick as gravy on biscuits. Her voice was deeper than I expected but was warm and friendly. She sounded nervous. Who wouldn't be? I certainly was.

"Oh, Sheila," she gushed, "Ah am so happy that you wanted to do this. Ah begged Adam's dad to let me talk with you, but he just said you would be too upset. Ah hope you are not upset. Ah don't want you to be upset. Really Ah don't. Adam's dad tells me so many wonderful things about you—how he admires you as a mother and that you are the best darn teacher he has eva known. Ah neva hear men talk that way about their ex-wives. Down here—well, it's just heinous. Everybody always has their panties in a wad ova something or otha. My Gawd, if my son's daddy eva gets outta jail, well, Ah just know that the first thing he'll do is try to separate me from mah boy. Now, Ah don't want you to worry. There's no way he will get anywhere near Adam." She pronounced *Adam* with a long A. She went on and on—it was a perfectly prepared monologue. "And Nana and Pop-pah—them's mah parents—they are just so tickled to meet Adam too. There's a whole slew of us just ready to welcome him to Buford."

"Buford?"

"Oh—we don't actually live in At-lanna—it's just easier to describe where we live by telling people that we live in At-lanna. You understand. Ah knew you would."

I did not know whether to be amused or frightened. This was a whole new level of conversation for me. Not just the ex-wife to the girlfriend thing—but the California to the Southern thing.

"Mandy, let me get a word in here, okay?" I felt austere, cold, firm, not how I wanted to feel at all. Deep breaths, deep breaths. And then the words came. From where or whom, I do not know, but if Mandy had written a script for me, it couldn't have been better.

"As I am sure you can appreciate"—damn, if my articulation didn't sound snooty in comparison—"this is not an easy conversation for me—probably not for either of us. And what Adam's dad is asking of me is a big deal—a really big deal."

"Ah know, honey," she interrupted. "If my son's fatha asked me to let him take our boy across the country, Ah'd tell him he's hafta kill me first. And he might just take that as a request—not a threat. I swear, that bastard is not comin' anywhere near us—that son of a bitch."

I liked her already. She spoke my language.

"So here is what I would like to happen." A pause and a sigh. "I know who I am dealing with when it comes to Adam's dad—what he can do, what he can't do, how much he can handle—you know what I mean. And I wish you the best with him, I really do. There is nothing that I want more for him than to be happy. And that is all I am going to say about him." Another pause and sigh. "Now, you are a mother and I am a mother, and the only way I can talk to you *is* mother to mother. I must know—I must feel completely safe and comfortable that you are going to be able to take care of the most precious and vulnerable person in my life. Mother to mother—this is the conversation we are having. Are you okay with this?"

"Okay?" she yelped. "This could not be more perfect. Ah was prayin' and prayin' that we could just talk like girlfriends, so you have mah word—mother to mother. Yes, ma'am."

That first phone conversation lasted a little over an hour and true to our word, we spoke strictly as mother to mother. As much as the petty, small, jealous parts of me wanted to hate her, I must say, that the lilt in her voice when she spoke about her son, her warmth when sharing the many "edifying" (*hah!*) things she would plan for Adam, stories of her own parents, her grandma Mizz Mussure, her sisters and life in Buford touched me and allowed me to relax. At one point during our conversation, Adam came into the room, and typical of Adam, he was droning. Mandy's response was what assured me more than anything else that my son would be safe in her care. "Oh," she interjected, "is that Adam? Ah know it is—that noise is a comfort to me. So many of my students make those stimming noises. Having Adam here will be just like school, my second home."

We had a few conversations over the next few weeks, and I really must hand it to Mandy, she kept the contents and confidentiality of those conversations between the two of us—mother to mother. She did have an expertise in autism, and she was excited to be able to share it with my son and with me. She wanted to help our lives become easier. She also offered my son something that I had always prayed for—an extended family who was ready to embrace him. Adam did go the Buford that December, and all was well.

I slept.

Mandy and Adam's dad eloped to Vegas in April 2004 and in June, the caravan arrived to move him back to Buford, Georgia. It was the first time I met her in person, and she was nothing like I thought she would be. That little Southern belle turned out to be a rather large woman who towers over Adam's dad. She dwarfs me considerably. Yet, within her ample frame lies the largest and most generous heart you could ever want to know. She *is* Southern hospitality. And what I love most, she is a strong woman—there is no messing around with Mandy. I wanted her on our team. I felt like

Baptista Minola, Kate's father in *Taming of the Shrew*, inwardly giggling when he realized that his out-of-control daughter had met her match. "Good luck to ya, Adam's dad!"

And that is why in June 2004, Adam traveled with the newlyweds and the Joads in that two-truck caravan across the United States to At-lanna. Adam got to know his new stepmom, stepbrother, grandparents, and cousins. It most certainly made the trip more difficult for them, and for a man who was trying to escape these responsibilities, it took courage for them to add Adam to their travels. I know that this was her plan. This is a woman who will always get what she wants.

Mandy, who as promised, reached out to me, mom to mom, and sent me pictures of Adam at the Grand Canyon, Adam at Carlsbad Caverns, Adam at the Alamo, and Adam at Graceland. She was right on all counts; it was an *edifying* experience for him in so many important ways. And for the first time ever, I had a break. I did not know how badly I needed one.

Mandy has been in our lives for over fifteen years now. I appreciate her more than ever.

She offers tremendous support to Adam and generous support to me.

She is the coparent I always needed.

And I, who swore I would never go to Buford, Georgia, have taken Adam to see his dad numerous times because it is good for Adam. I got to put Adam's needs ahead of mine in the most important way, even though I would have rather behaved like an angry, out-of-control abandoned wife and mother.

Mandy decorated the guest room in Buford especially for me. She has taken me to Buford's version of the Whistle Stop Café and made sure that I tasted authentic fried green tomatoes. She even sat with me on Aunt Piddy Pat's Porch where we drank mint juleps so that I could have a real live taste of *Gone with the Wind*. Sadly, the juleps were ghastly; they looked like swamp water with a stalk of seaweed coming out of them. And Mandy will corroborate this. So much for the charm of the Old South.

Mother to mother, Mandy has made it comfortable to consult with her, and by putting aside my hurt ego and pride, I have learned to seek her input on Adam. She held my hand when I knew that it was better for Adam to have independence and move into group home, reviewing our options and giving me advice. She helps me interview his job coaches and is unafraid to challenge things that I might have missed.

Mandy was a tiger mom before there was any such label. And because she has an objectivity that I will never possess, she helps me raise my son from three thousand miles away. When it comes to planning for Adam, I feel closer to her than anyone else. She was not afraid to jump in and be part of this family. Conversely, I have been able to offer her insight and suggestions to help her with her son as he navigated his high school and college years. It has been a good reciprocation of educational and parental support.

Sure, there have been times of stress and conflict when I lost assurance of my place in the world. But that was not Mandy's fault. She was elevated to sainthood by Adam's dad's family when the only way they could rationalize their son's divorce, second only to the shame of having to handle the first member of the family diagnosed with autism (six members of the family have since been identified on the ASD), they eagerly marginalized me by saying, "Thank God for Mandy—Adam would be nowhere if Mandy hadn't come into his life." It devastated me to be so flagrantly discounted and marginalized as a mom.

And even though there are still times when Adam's dad inserts himself and messes things up, Mandy helps me to understand that his intentions are good, as good as intentions can be from a man who moved three thousand miles away from his sons and only sees them two times per year.

It can't be easy for him—having to deal with both his current wife *and* his ex-wife when we discuss what is best for Adam. I feel some small pleasure of poetic justice that his current wife and his ex-wife share mutual care and respect for one another. We are an unusual family.

I have had the opportunity of observing their marriage both close-up and from afar for many years, and although I do not ask questions or offer advice, I know who he is and what she deals with. I was married to the man for almost twenty years. And thanks to Mandy, I now understand why I felt so crazy so much of the time. The difference is that she refuses to put up with his passive-aggressive shit, where I lived in fear of it. But that is another story, and truthfully, no longer any of my business. I have full confidence that Mandy will quickly put an end to that!

Oh yes, there are times I want to get even, to hold on to past hurts and resentments to keep that bad dad from winning. I still seek a world that is fair and just and where the nice people can win—for once. But back to the need for acceptance—this is not how life works.

So I ask myself, *Who really wins and who really loses if I hold on to the hurt?* I would be lying not to confess that I do believe there is a special place in hell for a man who moves three thousand miles away from his autistic son. And even more unrealistically, I still hold a sliver of hope that someday he might come back and simply apologize for how much he hurt us.

But deep down, I know that this is never going to happen.

I simply remember who I am dealing with, and fortunately, I *can* deal with Mandy.

Mandy and Me, Summer 2016

Had I understood his limitations and maybe accept that Adam's dad may also lie somewhere on the spectrum, perhaps we could have avoided being part of the divorce statistic. But for all that did and did not happen between Adam's dad and me, no apology is needed today. Like Josh said, "Mom, it was over long before it was over." Or something like that.

Holding on to the hurt keeps me from moving on, and if I stop growing, I will not be the kind of mother I want to be for Adam.

I ask myself, how much pain must have Adam's dad felt, how miserable must he have been with life to give up even one day with his son? He must have felt miserable about himself to have been able to do that. I do not wish this kind of pain and anguish upon anyone

No matter how angry you are and how much you have been hurt, the day will come when you wake up and realize that when a person behaves badly and does hurtful things, he is not doing anything to you; he is behaving in a way that speaks volumes about how he feels about himself. When you realize this, there is a possibility that his new wife can become your friend and ally.

I am proud of the relationship I have with Mandy. I respect her. I trust her. I am grateful for her. Few people understand how we can achieve this—or why. I cannot imagine it any other way.

If Mandy and I stay committed to our initial conversation where we set up the terms of our relationship—mother to mother— then we are able to figure out, hold fast and more forward with what is best for Adam.

And Adam is worth so much more than anything that ever happened in the past.

Welcome to Holland

I am often asked to describe the experience of raising a child with a disability - to try to help people who have not shared that unique experience to understand it, to imagine how it would feel. It's like this...

When you're going to have a baby, it's like planning a fabulous vacation trip - to Italy. You buy a bunch of guide books and make your wonderful plans. The colliseum. The Michaelangelo David. The gondolas in Venice. You may learn some handy phrases in Italian. It's all very exciting.

After months of eager anticipation, the day finally arrives. You pack your bags and off you go. Several hours later, the plane lands. The stewardess comes in and says, "Welcome to Holland."

"Holland?!?" you say. "What do you mean, "Holland"??? I signed up for Italy! I'm supposed to be in Italy. All my life I dreamed of going to Italy."

But there's been a change in the flight plans. They've landed in Holland and there you must stay.

The important thing is that they haven't taken you to a horrible, disgusting, filthy place, full of pestilence, famine and disease. It's just a different place.

So you must go and buy new guide books. And you must learn a whole new language. And you will meet a whole new group of people you never would have met.

It's just a different place. It's slower than Italy, less flashy than Italy. But after you've been there for awhile and you catch your breath, you look around... and you begin to notice that Holland has windmills... Holland has tulips. Holland even has Rembrandts.

But everyone you know is busy coming and going from Italy... and they're all bragging about what a wonderful time they had there. And for the rest of your life, you will say, "Yes, that's where I was supposed to go. That's what I had planned."

And the pain of that will never, ever, ever, ever go away... because the loss of that dream is a very significant loss.

But... if you spend your life mourning the fact that you didn't get to Italy, you may never be free to enjoy the very special, the very lovely things... about Holland. ~Emily Perl Kingsley

Source material: https://www.google.com/
search?q=italy+holland+story+special+needs&source
Reprinted with permission from Emily Perl Kinglsey (copyright 1987)

It is with much sorrow that I must share that since writing this chapter, Mandy and I have parted ways. After fourteen years of working together, Mandy now must prioritize challenges brought on by Adam's dad's medical conditions. Mandy must put his needs above Adam's, which has led to conflicts in how to best care for Adam. We are no longer able have "'mother to mother'" levels of interaction. I miss her—very much.

CHAPTER 12

Don't Leave Home Without It!

There have been many adventures on this journey with Adam, and I frequently look back and ask myself, "What was I thinking?" Over the years I have learned to be gentle with myself and accept that I was valiantly, or perhaps merely, only doing the best that I could under the circumstances under which I was living, but the 2002 trip to Las Vegas and subsequent Hummer trip to the southern ridge of the Grand Canyon definitely falls under the category "What was I thinking?" More correctly, "Was I out of my mind?"

We had officially been a family of three for eight months, and this would be the first spring break that we did not have a family vacation planned. One of the more irrational promises I made to myself was that my sons would not feel any loss in our lifestyle even though we were now a broken family, and so I planned for us an exciting trip to Las Vegas. And because I was determined that they not think I was incapable of providing for them on my own, I over-compensated for everything. So not only were Josh, Adam, and I going to take a five-day vacation to Las Vegas, Josh invited his two closest friends, Aaron J. and Jamie, to join us. One mom, four sons, one of whom is severely autistic. Yep, I was into self-flagellation. I figured that it would be fun for Josh to have his friends with him and that, as a threesome, they would be safe going to all the fun activities that Vegas now offered for families and teens. What did I know? Apparently, not much. We stayed in a seasonal resort "off the strip" with pools and large-screen TVs, walking distance to the "family friendly" events and just far enough not to be inundated with the gambling, partying, and drinking of Vegas fame. Vegas was reinventing itself—a place for family fun—so why not go?

This adventure seemed like a perfect get-away for Adam. He loves riding in the car and is a great passenger. The movement of driving down the highway, the humming of the wheels, nonstop playing of his favorite Disney music to which Josh, Aaron J., Jamie, and I happily sang along, being able to swim twenty-four hours a day or night at the resort, being with his brother, room service, and unlimited in-room cartoons and movies, a fifteen-year-old autistic boy's definition of heaven. This trip would be the first time that the boys and I were not invited to join his dad's family on their annual family vacation, so I wanted it to feel special for us all. For the past six years, our spring vacation destination had been to the Palm Desert Marriott Resort where the boys' dad's parents rented suites for all five of their children, spouses, and seven grandchildren. It was our first experience of learning that being divorced means that the entire family divorces you. I think I expected that the boys and I would still be a welcomed part of the family. But as the saying goes, blood is thicker than water, and since the boy's dad was off on one of his rendezvous with one of his online girlfriends, part of his newfound freedom as a once again single man, he would not be taking the boys to Palm Desert. I had to come up with a great plan to reduce the anxiety Adam was experiencing with this drastic departure from what he had come to know as the family vacation to Palm Desert. With Adam, once "it" is on the calendar, he expects that "it" will be repeated every year for the next eight thousand years. I would deal with 2003 when it got here.

The five-hour drive was a straight shot down I-15. Our days and nights were well-planned; water park one day, the family package at Circus Circus another, tickets to see the Blue Man Group and Cirque du Soleil, discount tickets for endless all-you-can-eat buffets where the boys gorged on what they thought were gourmet meals, and Adam enjoyed an endless supply of grilled cheese sandwiches, french fries, and lemonade. And included in our "package of family fun" was an action-packed adventure in a Hummer Jeep to the South Rim of the Grand Canyon. On day 3 of our Las Vegas vacation, we awoke at 5:30 a.m. to be on time for our 6:15 a.m. departure from the MGM Grand Hotel. The brochure had advertised this:

Your gold rush adventure begins as we travel in comfort to historic Nelson Nevada. You will pass petrified sand dunes, extinct volcanoes, and colorful geological formations in the most powerful, safest off-road vehicle ever built—Hummer! Then the excitement continues as the powerful Hummer travels deep into the desert on old mining trails not accessible by ordinary vehicles. After a stunning view of the famous Colorado River, your guide will serve you a sumptuous lunch as you dine at the South Rim of the Grand Canyon. Total time: 6.5 hours.

As promised—our guide and the Hummer arrived at the MGM promptly at 6:15. I was excited, Adam was compliant, while Josh, Aaron J., and Jamie willingly went along for the sheer entertainment of it all. Our guide and the Hummer were waiting for us. We were each handed our bottle of water and introduced to the other members of our Adventure Party. There were twelve in all—including the driver. In addition to the five of us, we met the wife and son of Álvaro García Linera, who at the time was the Bolivian ambassador to the United States. Neither Senora Linera nor little Eduardo spoke English, which thrilled Josh, Aaron J., and Jamie as an opportunity to practice their Spanglish throughout the trip. Senora Linera was a beautiful Latina, dressed in her red wool suit and black high-heeled shoes. Eduardo looked like he had just stepped out of the private Catholic school that he attended in DC. Also joining us on our Grand Canyon Adventure was the Smith Family from Bossier City, Louisiana. There was the dad, Mr. Dalton Smith ("But y'all can call me Big D"), the mom, Tully Smith ("Y'all can call her Ma"), their fifteen-year-old daughter, Jamie ("Hey"), and Jamie's best friend, Jamie. Yep, three Jamies in a Hummer; the girls could not get over that a boy was named Jamie. Ma was fascinated by Adam, and Big D climbed up front into the passenger's seat with our driver and guide, Gunnery Sergeant Scott O'Mally USMC Desert Storm, who completed the dozen. After our "Buenos dias" and "Howdy" greetings, the rest of us climbed into the back of the Hummer where we immediately realized, there were no windows except the little peephole at the back of the Jeep. We were tightly fit and claustrophobic, but we were all in good spirits and ready for our big adventure. "*Shit*, I forgot to bring Adam's meds." This realization sent me into a panic that I could not let anyone see. I quickly did the math: "Six and a half hours, it's six thirty, we will be back by two at the latest, next dose is not until 4:00 p.m., we should be fine." I relaxed.

The excursion to the South Rim was filled with conversation and fun. We all tried speaking in Spanish to Senora Linera, who pleasantly smiled at us, but who must have been secretly thinking that we were all morons. Tally and I swapped stories of raising teens, comparing life in Louisiana to life in California. Adam was content looking out the little window at the back of the Hummer. And Josh, Aaron J., and (boy) Jamie, all three of whom were on the Comedy Sportz Team at their high school, kept us entertained by playing an assortment of improv games. According to the schedule, we would arrive at the South Rim at 10:00 a.m. At around 10:45 a.m., I knocked on the window separating the passengers in the back from the front cab of the Hummer and inquired, "Sergeant Scott, are we going to get there soon? I need to use the bathroom."

"Mama," said daughter Jamie, "she said bathroom."

"She means lavatory, darlin'," replied Ma.

"They shore do talk differ'nt out here, don't they?" added friend Jamie.

"Well, ladies, I don't want you to fret," said Sergeant Scott, "but this is my first solo trip out here and I missed the turnoff about an hour ago. Got it under control now. Heading back—then we'll get on that ol' mining trail—just relax and enjoy the scenery." Who was he kidding; we did not have any windows back here and Adam was not going to give up his view out the one window in the back of the Hummer to let any of the rest of us look out.

The boys continued playing improv games. Tully was looking at my neck in a curious manner. She whispered something to daughter Jamie, who whispered something to friend Jamie, and then all three stared at my neck. Trying to be subtle, I felt around my neck, chest, and shoulders to see if there was a spider crawling on me. Nothing.

"Miss Sheila," inquired Tully Smith, "I don't mean to be rude, but I hafta ask you. Is that one of those Jewish stars hangin' around your pretty little neck?"

I looked at Josh, Aaron J, and Jamie. We tried to suppress our nervous laughter.

"Why, yes, Tully, it is a star of David."

Tully reached over and banged on the window to the cab. "Big D, Big D! You are not going to believe this. We got ourselves some bona fide Jews here."

Big D whipped his head around so fast that he pulled a muscle in his back. He stared at Josh, Aaron J., boy Jamie, Adam and me. "You tellin' me that you are all Jews?" he belted in disbelief.

"Oh my god!" shrieked the two Jamie girls. "Mama, I've never seen Jews before!"

"Que paso? Que paso?" asked a worried Senora Linera.

"Somos Judío," inserted a proud Aaron J.

"De verdad?"

"Si, en verdad," Josh, Aaron J. and Jamie replied in unison. They do that—improv training.

"Mama!" shrieked daughter Jamie. "I didn't know that Jews could speak Spanish."

Big D demanded that Gunnery Sergeant Scott O'Mally USMC Desert Storm pull the Hummer over immediately.

What the heck?

"I gotta stretch, son. Wrenched my back. Tully, don't you scare me like that again."

Honestly, I thought that the five of us were going to be dropped off right there in the middle of nowhere because we were Jewish. And all I could think of was, "*Shit,* I forgot Adam's meds."

"Good idea," said Sergeant Scott, "I need to get my bearings. Why don't we all get out and take a stretch? But careful of the scorpions, folks."

We finally arrived at the South Rim around 12:30 p.m., and unbelievably, it was closed! *Closed!* Who closes the Grand Canyon? All around the viewing areas and paths to hike down into the canyon was that orange barrier safety fencing, and we could get nowhere near the beautiful views we had hoped to hike down to and see. Sergeant Scott pulled out a couple of loaves of white bread, some peanut butter and jelly, bags of Lays potato chips, and some Oreos, and we each prepared our gourmet lunch at the picnic tables that had been placed at the location for our enjoyment.

It was about this time that Josh became a little cranky—no, really pissed at me for planning such a ludicrous trip when they could have all been back at the resort sleeping or swimming or watching TV. Truthfully, I felt the same way, but as the adult in the group, I was the one who had to hold it together if only to keep Adam calm. The clock was ticking on his-time released meds, and I did not want to add any fuel to the fire. At least we hadn't been left to wander, as were our ancestors, in the Mojave Desert.

We were about an hour into the drive back to Vegas when the Hummer broke down. My first thought was that we had run out of gas, you know, with Sergeant Scott having missed the turn off and all, but after Big D and Sergeant Scott had examined the engine, they declared "Yep—sumthins definitely busted" but I had no idea what.

There was no cell phone reception that far off the grid, so we were basically stranded. Gunnery Sergeant Scott used his Desert Storm experience to outline for us "what would happen" and we all had to obey *his* orders. Everyone had to stay in the Hummer; we had two gallons of water that we would divide up and share. Fortunately, we all had our empty bottles with us. Next, we would wait for someone to drive by. We would flag them down, give them the phone number of the Tour Company, and have them call the owner for us when they reached the main road and had cell reception. Sergeant Scott collected money from us to give those people we hoped would drive by as a reward for helping us. Aaron J. was doing his best to translate all this into Spanish. Next, we would wait for the owner of the company to arrive with another Hummer into which we would all climb and then be safely delivered into the parking lot of the MGM Grand Hotel.

I was curious about the contingency plan—*just in case no one drove by.* Sergeant Scott assured us that if he did not return the Hummer by 7:00 p.m. that the owner of the Tour Company would get into his helicopter and come looking for us. Not to worry. He then proceeded to tell us a few stories of being stranded in Afghanistan and how the US Marine Corps will never leave a man behind. "Hoo-yah!"

Daughter Jamie and friend Jamie began to cry. They were tired and fatigued from all the delays. More importantly, the Louisiana Smiths had 7:30 p.m. tickets to see Siegfried and Roy at the Mirage Hotel. "Mama, we did not come all the way to Las Vegas to miss those tigers."

Adam had begun to drone. "What is he doin', Mama?"

"Sorry, ma'am, you cannot take him out of the Jeep to walk around."

It was just about that time when Josh, Aaron J. and Jamie (boy) decided to begin writing their screenplay for *Final Destination: Terror in the Desert.* The most fun was in their casting of the movie:

Eleven tourists board a Hummer Jeep driven by former Marine Gunnery Sergeant, Scott O'Mally (Matt Damon) on a tour to the South Rim of the Grand Canyon. As they climb into the back of the Hummer bound for the South Rim, Aaron J. (Keanu Reeves) has a premonition that the Hummer will break down in the middle of the Mojave Desert, leaving the tourist passengers to be killed off one by one. When the events from his vision begin to repeat themselves in reality, Aaron J. panics, and a fight breaks out, which leads to the rest of the passengers being left behind including Josh (Jack Black), Jamie (Will Farrell), Big D. (Russell Crowe), Ma Tully (Sissy Spacek), daughter Jamie (Kirstin Dunst), friend Jamie (Amanda Peet), Senora Linera and Little Eduardo (Salma Hayek and Nick Jonas), and Adam and me. Haley Joel Osment got cast as Adam, and no matter how much I pleaded for Debra Messing, I was being portrayed by Kathy Bates. Through a series of bizarre accidents, the survivors begin to die one by one and Josh attempts to find a way to "cheat" death's plan before it's too late. Six weeks later, the owner of the Tour Company finally arrives by helicopter to find that only Adam has survived. Being autistic, Adam had no fear of death and was completely unaware of what was happening to those around him. Because he has been without his meds for six weeks, Adam crushes the owner by banging him on the head with a giant neon Las Vegas sign, and climbs into the helicopter to be flown back to the MGM Grand Hotel. As the final credits roll, Adam can be heard saying, "Helicopter, up in the sky!"

Obeying every detail of Sergeant Scott's plan, sure enough, after three hours, a car did drive by which he flagged down, and the two young men agreed to take the $253 collected and call the owner of the Tour Company for us. They also agreed to take Ma Smith, daughter Jamie, and friend Jamie back with them so that they would not have to miss the Siegfried and Roy show. As dusk began to fall, Sergeant Scott had the rest of us climb out of the Hummer and up on top of the roof because, as he put it, "The rattlesnakes come out at night folks and they have been known to crawl inside the cabin." He helped us to the top of the roof, and I was duly impressed that even though she had to take off her high heels, Senora Linera did not get a run in her nylons. Big D was still having back spasms from having turned around so quickly in his seat to look at the real live Jews and he bravely volunteered to remain on the ground with Sergeant Scott to protect us from the rattlesnakes. Had it been me, I would have been far more worried about having my wife, my daughter, and my daughter's best friend getting into a car with two complete strangers, but then again, I have never lived in the South. Sergeant Scott made us all feel that much safer and secure when he pulled out his ATI FX45 GI semiauto 1911 Pistol from under the driver's seat and fired off a shot to assure us that no rattlesnake would get past him. By that point, I wanted Adam's meds for myself.

We did finally get rescued by the owner of the Tour Company, who was later cast to be played by George Carlin, and we arrived back at the parking lot of the MGM Grand Hotel around 10:00 p.m. The two Jamies came running up with their souvenir picture of Siegfried and Roy, and all were happily reunited.

The biggest miracle of that adventure was that despite missing his four o'clock and seven o'clock meds, Adam did not have a meltdown during the entire day or night. Yes, we were tired and yes, we were hungry. And yes, I had to promise Josh that I would *never* plan a trip like that for us again, but other than that, we all came out unscathed and with a great screenplay!

Since the early days when Dr. Looney suggested that we start Adam on his meds, I have been hypervigilant in making sure that he receives them as scheduled. The day of the adventure to the South Rim of the Grand Canyon was the first time I had failed. And yet on that day, everything was fine. This was in stark contrast to the time we were peacefully driving in the car and then out of nowhere, Adam blew up, grabbed my arm, and bit it so ferociously that it was a miracle that I did not cause a major accident on the freeway. And in another incident while waiting calmly on line at the pharmacy he exploded and pushed me to the ground, then attacked three others waiting for the line to move, necessitating that the LAPD be called to harness him. Of course, by the time they arrived, the incident was long over. These are the risks of going out in public with Adam: will he or will he not explode? And the mystery is that, we do not see it coming. In Adam speak, he calls it "Volcano," which makes perfect sense. I have begun to accept that in these instances, my son is the Incredible Hulk. Except the Hulk warns others not "…to make me mad," whereas Adam cannot.

The overarching concern regardless of what we plan, must always be, "Will Adam be able to handle this situation?" followed by "and how can I best prepare him?" Like Gunnery Sergeant Scott O'Mally, I must always have an initial and then a contingency plan. I know the importance of walking Adam through what is going to happen before it happens, and as I learned from the Grand Canyon Adventure, to always be ready for the unexpected. Thus far, however, I have yet to hide an ATI FX45 GI semiauto 1911 Pistol under the driver's seat of my car.

Long ago I made the decision that autistic or not, married or not, my vow as a parent is to provide my sons with joyful lives filled with fun and adventure. For Adam's sixteenth birthday (2003), we went up in a hot air balloon. Why, because that is what we did for Josh. And when he turned twenty-one (2008), we went river rafting on the American River South Fork. It was while floating down the American River that I understood, "Now isn't this exactly what life with Adam is about?" Every morning we get into our raft. Sometimes the water is clear and calm. And sometimes, right around the corner, is a class 5 rapid. You just don't know what is coming next. What I do need to know is how to navigate the river wherever it leads us. The best I can do is use my experience, follow my instincts and do all that I can to ensure that everyone is safe. That is why we wear life vests. Sometimes on our backs. Sometimes in the raft. And sometimes, just by making sure we take our meds.

CHAPTER 13

Legalization

In July 2005, Adam turned eighteen. It is so hard to believe how fast the years had flown.

I had been a single mom for four years now, and to be honest, I had yet to really adjust to this new status. Josh was finishing his first year of college, and Adam would be moving from his high school program into the final stage, the transition program, where over the next four years, he would prepare to leave the educational system and move into the real world. When we had our first IEP at age three, and I could not begin to imagine Adam at age six or age nine or age twelve; I certainly had no vision of my son at age eighteen. But here we were.

Turning eighteen means many things. It means new privileges and freedoms. It means you are legally treated as an adult. You can now enjoy certain rights along with the requirement to fulfill certain duties including voting, getting a tattoo, being called up by the selective service, buying a lottery ticket, leasing an apartment, getting married, obtaining a credit card, going to jail, gambling, and most of all, no longer being protected by your parents. I will let you decide whether these are privileges or burdens. And this is true for every minor who turns eighteen—unless you are an eighteen-year-old who cannot make any of these decisions for yourself. It specifically affects the parents of children with special needs, for we need to consider if we want to continue being fully responsible for our now chronologically, but not developmentally, adult child. I was daunted that Adam was becoming an adult, however, I was certain that he would not be capable of making any adult decisions for himself. And so began the next phase of our lives: having to accept that my now eighteen-year old son with autism could not be given the rights and responsibilities that come with adulthood. The big, legal term for this is called conservatorship.

Becoming a conservator was the next item on the list of "Things I Never Knew I Would Have to Know." There was never a moment's hesitation about whether to conserve Adam. He is our son and whether we were married or not, I had not a thought that we would not always be his parents. I was certain Mandy was standing next to me. *"Ha! Don't assume what you don't know, Sheila."* Two more shocking realities were added to my already shaken-up world. The first was that now that he was eighteen, Adam's dad was no longer legally required to pay any child support. I should not have been surprised when Adam's dad immediately stopped paying this, nor should I have been so upset as I realized we would never see another penny from him again. After all, money for Josh had stopped the day his dad moved to Georgia—less than twenty-four hours after Josh graduated from high school in June 2004. How did I miss this in our divorce settlement? Again, it was nowhere on my radar that his dad would not continue financial support. He may have wanted to be away from me, but our sons?

Second, I was speechless when informed by his dad that he did not want to share conservatorship of Adam. He feared having any legal responsibility for whatever might happen in the future. *"What if we are sued? We could lose our homes or our savings."*

Oh, Mandy, you let me down! You put a price on Adam.

Every pain of the divorce resurfaced, another abandonment. I returned to anguished disbelief that his dad was done with us—really *done.* Not with criticizing me as a person, not with gaslighting my sense of self, not with being the fun dad who flew into California twice a year—but *done* with any accountability for the legal, financial, medical, recreational, housing, or work-related needs of our son.

Another slap into reality—I am truly on my own. Happy eighteenth birthday, Adam.

So what to do? One more time I suited up, put on my big girl pants, and leapt into this new world called "conservatorship."

There were many steps to the process, and I had heard the many horror stories of lack of understanding, tedious meetings, house visits, and judgment that accompany getting conservatorship. I am happy to report that none of this was our experience because what I learned to value and appreciate was that each step of the process was designed to protect Adam from any person or agency that might potentially take advantage of his resources.

I could have been insulted or offended that my integrity was being challenged by the legal system as if I had some ulterior motive for collecting my son's SSI. No, the purpose is to ensure that Adam, or any adult with a severe disability, is not being denied his inalienable rights as an adult and to prevent him from being exploited, even by his mom. Look, we all watch *The People's Court*, right? We know how crazy families can become. We borrow and refuse to pay back; we hit and run; we lie, change the narrative, and even abscond funds. Family court has no shortage of stories that give us reason to pause. And so, Adam and I began the necessary steps to have the State of California declare my son "legally incompetent."

It sounds so unsavory, unappealing, and demeaning to have a person labeled "legally incompetent," and it broke my heart to have to utter these words. The other option would have been not to petition for conservatorship, at which point, Adam would become a "ward of the state" and that possibility would never be an option. I know, Mandy would tell me, "Sheila, never say never," but as long as I am on this planet, I know that I am the best (and now the only) person to be making decisions for my son. Words, words, words—I had to let go of the legalese and do what I knew in my heart to be the right thing for my son.

As background, a "limited" conservatorship was specifically developed by the California legislature on behalf of developmentally disabled adults, wherein it provides for a broad range of conservatorship powers from medical decision making to the fullest range of powers depending upon the severity of the "adult's" disabilities. That is, a limited conservatorship is tailored to the needs of the disabled. These "powers" are obtained and granted to the conservator. A limited conservator may be granted the authority to do the following:

- Decide where the conservatee will live.
- Manage the conservatee's social affairs.
- Manage the conservatee's financial affairs.
- Examine the conservatee's confidential records and papers.
- Sign a contract on behalf of the conservatee.
- Give or withhold consent for medical treatments.
- Make decisions regarding education and vocational training.

Obtaining a limited conservatorship requires the completion of numerous court-ordered forms, regional center intervention, an attorney appointed to represent your adult child, a court-ordered investigator, plus court appearances. A special needs law practice manages the entire process.

OBTAINING A CONSERVATORSHIP—THE PROCESS

A conservatorship is granted in a court proceeding where a superior court judge appoints a responsible person (a conservator) to care for another adult (a conservatee) who cannot care for themselves or their finances.

After the filing of a petition for limited conservatorship, a proposed limited conservatee is assessed at a regional center to determine if the proposed conservatee is indeed developmentally disabled. The regional center submits a written report of its findings and recommendations regarding the conservatorship to the court. While the regional center report is not binding, it provides the court with guidance about the appropriateness of the conservatorship. In Adam's case, regional center forwarded sixteen years of records. There was much to read.

Additionally, the court appoints an attorney and an investigator to represent the disabled adult in court to make certain that the proposed conservatorship is with merit. Typically, the entire process of obtaining a conservatorship is completed within forty-five to ninety days after filing the petition depending upon the county in which the court is located, local practices/policies, and timeframe for obtaining a hearing date. As the petitioner, I was also required to secure a lawyer to represent me and my desire to conserve my son.

Paying the retainer of $2,500, the attorney arranged for all the necessary interviews and court documentations to determine if indeed Adam was significantly disabled enough to be rendered *legally incompetent*. I had to be willing to agree and accept the findings of the court, what they may or may not be and to what extent. Would I be granted many or few "powers" for his needs? I was required to attend numerous training sessions at the superior court to learn about the extent of my role, the limits of my role, when I would simply be *Mom* and when I would be required to put on my *conservator* hat. What I learned at the training sessions had more to do with the depth and breadth of what potential conservators and families have had to endure and how easy I had it compared to others. It was humbling. I met families who were also petitioning for conservatorship not only for their child with a disability but those who were taking over responsibility for their aging parents or their mentally ill siblings. The stories—what people live with—I felt lucky to only be dealing with autism. There was the sister who was seeking conservatorship over her brother, a child rapist, who was fighting for him *not* being released from jail. She was afraid for the safety of the children he had been stalking should her brother be back on the streets. And then there were the siblings who were trying to protect their senile parents from being exploited by nursing homes or smarmy financial advisors, who had already swindled away hundreds of thousands of dollars in Ponzi schemes and retirement frauds. Stress and tears filled the workshops as people unburdened their circumstances to the officers of the courts. It was a surreal circus of angst, distress and fears as people fought to protect their loved ones or society. And the representatives of the courts had to assess if the requests were legitimate or not. As an observer of other families' tales, it was hard to discern if the stories were true or not—I hoped that these people had good intentions but had secret suspicions that some were also part of the scam. I mean, who would want to sit through these types of meetings if they did not have to? But then again, if there was a lot of money at stake... This was an education unto itself, and like I said, it made autism seem easy.

Three caseworkers were assigned to Adam and me, each of whom would be coming to visit us in our home to interview Adam. Their goal was to determine if Adam truly needed to be conserved, if I was responsible and honest enough to be his conservator, if I knew how to work with and not against the system—and then to verify that I was not trying to deprive Adam's father of having access to his now adult son. That last part burned deeply, yet through these interviews, I developed a healthy respect for the system. When wearing those big girl pants rather than bemoaning the audacity of it all, I was able to accept the importance of a system that was designed to protect my son. I got to practice getting out of my own way.

The first interview was from the Regional Center. It was conducted by our own caseworker with whom we had been working since 2001. Nikki knew Adam and our family well, and she had all of Adam's records since we first began testing in 1989. The Regional Center (Nikki) submitted a written report of her findings and recommendations regarding the conservatorship to the court. While the regional center report was not binding, it provided the court with guidance about the appropriateness of my conservatorship request. I passed interview 1.

Next came the court appointed family law attorney and the social worker assigned to represent Adam in order to make certain that the proposed conservatorship had been requested with merit. The family law lawyer came to our home and asked to speak with

Adam privately. "Great," I replied, "I will be in the other room if you need me."

I could hardly wait to see how this would go. My hope was that Adam did not attack this young woman, but who knows, maybe that might have worked to our advantage. Trying not to be seen, I listened carefully.

"Hello, Adam. My name is _____. How are you today?"

"Winne the Pooh."

"Is this your home, Adam?"

"Christopher Robin, Piglet, Eeyore. Hundred-Acre Wood."

"Adam, Adam? What is your mother's name?"

"Kanga."

She did not know how to "speak Adam," but once you learn to "speak Adam," he communicates clearly:

"Hello Adam. My name is _____. How are you today?"

"Winne the Pooh." (*"Hurray for you. Hurray for me. Hurray, hurray."*)

"Is this your home, Adam?"

"Christopher Robin, Piglet, Eeyore. Hundred-Acre Wood." (*"You'll find the enchanted neighborhood of Christopher's childhood days."*)

Lyrics from "The Many Adventures of Winnie the Pooh" composed by Richard M. Sherman and Robert B. Sherman, source: http://www. disneyclips.com/lyrics/lyricspooh4.html.

"Adam, Adam? What is your mother's name?"

"Kanga." (No explanation needed.)

And then a pause.

"Sheila, could you come help out, please."

That was the end of the first interview.

A couple of weeks later the third court-appointed representative, the social worker, arrived to interview Adam. Once again, I was asked to leave the room so that she could speak with Adam privately. "Have at it!" I replied with a polite smile, and I once again left the room.

"Hello Adam. My name is _____.
How are you today?"

"Pizza snake."*

"How old are you, Adam."

"Adam 18—July 18—Adam out."

"Adam, Adam? Where is your father?"

"Daddy Georgia."

"Adam, do you want to live in California or Georgia?"

"Adam California. Mommy California. Daddy Georgia."

And then he got up and began to pace. And drone. And bite his finger. And hit his head.

My anxiety rose as I feared he would attack her, but I was not allowed to go back into the living room until I was summoned.

"Mrs.—, Adam needs you," the nervous social worker called out.

"Adam, knock it off," I snapped in my stern parental voice as I wrapped him in the weighted vest. It's what brings him back into consciousness of his surroundings.

Either this woman was a parent, or she was not.

Either she understood autism, or she did not.

Either she would report me as an abusive parent, or she would not.

I was just doing what I had done thousands of times throughout our lives to prevent my son from having a complete meltdown. I never knew if it would work or whether I would end up with another black eye. He was a big strong eighteen-year-old adult, and the best I could do was to intervene in hopes that none of us would get hit, bit, kicked, or tackled. Simple self-defense.

Once he gained composure, he would go into his next trope: "Camp Harmon, Easter Seals—Yes." Adam's fear was that if he acted out, he would be punished and lose a special outing. As if the meltdown itself wasn't already hard enough on him. I have chosen to believe that no matter how hard or embarrassing or even dangerous this may be for me, it is so much harder on Adam. As if he had any more control over these behaviors than he did over his breathing.

Just part of the autism—the not-so-pretty part. Let's be honest—the *awful* part of awtism.

"I am sorry you have to see this," I apologized to the social worker. "I just do not want him to escalate."

She looked stunned, having no idea what a total meltdown could look like.

In less than a minute, things returned to a state of calm. The look of terror relaxed from her face. She then explained that this was her first solo visit. I flashed back to our first meeting when Adam was entering developmental preschool. Once again, we were "a first."

"May I see his bedroom?" she asked. I was certain that she would be looking for straps and ties on the bedposts and barricades on the windows, her image of me having been so warped. Perhaps she was thinking that I really did feed him snake pizza. But no, all she found was a wonderful room—Adam's bed with the Tigger blanket, three bookcases filled with every Dr. Seuss, Disney story books, dictionaries in twenty languages, etc., his computer, his television, his dresser, and a closet filled with clean clothes. On the walls hung pictures of our family, framed drawings he had created, and two pictures painted by his brother. Was this a typical room for a young man of eighteen? No. Was it perfect for Adam with "Adam stuff"? Absolutely!

She asked to see the backyard and commented on the large play area and the beautiful jacuzzi complete with waterfall.

"Is he water safe?"

"Like a dolphin," I replied.

She checked the garage for safety, and luckily, I had remembered to hide the chainsaw and other torture devices that I used regularly on my son. I know I sound macabre, and I know that she was just doing her job, but honestly, how much did it take to see that I really love my son more than anything else in the world, and all I want is to take care of him, protect him, create a wonderful life for him?

We went back into the living room, and I asked if Adam could be excused to watch TV.

"Adam, remote."

She observed as Adam perfectly executed adult, man-cave control over the television.

She asked me a few questions about Adam's dad and informed me that the courts would also be contacting him to ascertain that it was his choice not to contest the conservatorship.

"Contest the conservatorship?" I meekly inquired. My heart and stomach sank.

"Oh yes," she replied as she began to wring her hands. Sometimes one parent tries to keep the other parent away from conservatorship.

"Trust me, he wants nothing to do with this."

"Then we should have no problem getting him to sign the papers."

"Sign the papers?"

Ha! She had no idea whom she would be trying to contact. *Good luck, lady.* More power to you if you can get Adam's dad to respond—in a timely manner. Inside I was spinning. How I wish getting him to sign the papers was the depth of my worries. She had no idea how difficult he could be. Remaining most business-like, she explained that Adam's dad has the right to contest the conservatorship until which point the legal conservator is appointed. The areas that might be contested include the following:

- Disputes regarding who should serve as the conservator
- Proposed conservatee objecting to the establishment of a conservatorship
- Removal of an existing conservator
- Visitation orders disputes
- Conservator not considering the reasonable wishes of the conservatee
- Modifying existing conservatorship powers
- Appointment of a successor conservator
- Co-conservators unable to make joint decisions

She shared that in contrast to conservatorships of elderly individuals where disputes often come between the children and siblings of the conservatee, in most cases with adults with special-needs, conservatorship disputes usually involve heated arguments between divorcing parents lashing out at one another.

I always wanted to believe that even though Adam's dad told me that he never loved me during our eighteen-year marriage, he was at least a good father who truly loved his sons. Well, as good a dad as one can be after moving three-thousand miles away. But I have already made this point—sorry, my resentment runs deep. It was just me that he did not love and whom he enjoyed making crazy. Really—the man derived pleasure out of seeing how upset I could become, and I excelled at taking the bait. But I trusted that he would never do anything ("Never say never," Mandy would tell me) that could be hurtful to his sons, especially Adam. The voice of the damaged woman who had been told that she had never been loved wreaked havoc in my head, causing me to fear that he would tell the courts that I was unstable or unfit to serve as Adam's conservator if only for his cynical enjoyment of hurting me more. After all, he had concrete evidence. I had been on antidepressants since he left us. I dreaded the possibility of having to fight for what I believed to be my moral and ethical responsibility for my son. From the conservator workshops at family court, I knew that a contested conservatorship could become very costly as well as emotionally draining. And for me, the emotional cost was the more dangerous of the two. But the law is the law, and because the law created this Catch-22, I provided the necessary contact information for Adam's dad and Mandy and did my best to keep myself from going into a full meltdown. Fear is a debilitating enemy. That night I tried on Adam's weighted vest to see if it would help me feel better.

A few weeks later, my lawyer called to inform me that the family courts had accepted our paperwork and interviews and all that was needed (prior to setting our court date) was the letter of release from Adam's dad. They had heard nothing. I was not surprised. "Could you please call him?" they asked. My lawyer advised me not to, concerned that it could be misinterpreted as trying to interfere with his decision.

I was devastated that Adam's dad would not join me as our son's conservators. Maybe it was yet another desperate attempt on my part to keep together what little we had left as a family. Maybe I doubted myself or simply did not want to be alone in making decisions for Adam. I still held onto the fantasy that we had at least parented well together. I needed that validation. I needed Mandy. Some of my friends suggested that this had nothing to do with Adam; it was yet another way of Adam's dad telling us he was done with us. Was I really that awful? Others suggested that he was just a cheap bastard whose love of money was greater than his love for his son. And still others told me to count my blessings that I would be free from him and that "Really, Sheila, you have always been doing this on your own anyways." I was reliving the deepest blows of rejection. And then my wise, older son confronted me.

"Mom, do you really think this matters to Adam?"

"It matters to me."

"I know, but this is not about you. It is about Adam. Do you really think this matters to him?"

Of course, it didn't. I just wanted to protect him from the rejection I felt. I want both my children to know how much they are loved, valued, wanted, respected, and cherished. No law can change this. Apparently, no legal paper can do this either.

"Mom," my supportive nineteen-year-old said, "you are enough."

I finally learned to effectively use one of Adam's dad's strategies to our advantage to get him to sign the paper work, albeit, I am not proud of having played this manipulative card. I told him that since I filed for conservatorship while Adam was still seventeen, that under California law, he would have to pay half of the legal costs, but if we received the papers within a week, I would not demand the money from him. Within days we received the signed forms. The costs never came up again.

I also received a series of emails from Adam's dad, or maybe they were actually written by Mandy, inquiring if I felt emotionally stable enough to take on this burden. Burden? Adam was never a burden. Challenging, yes, but I would not be who I am today if not for Adam. A mother's commitment is to walk with her children through every step of life. One child may not launch in the way most children do while the other one amazes you with insight and wisdom beyond his years, but to me, my children have been my greatest gift, never a burden, and I continue to feel blessed that they chose me to be their mom. I may be broken from the loss of my marriage, but we are still a family of three, a strong family, so I chose to listen to Josh's words and embrace that *I am enough.*

This was the last legal separation from Adam's dad, and it was long overdue.

The day finally came to go to court—July 20, 2005—two days after Adam turned eighteen. The week before I met with our lawyer to go over the terms of the limited conservatorship. The courts were granting me the rights to make decisions for Adam about housing, work, money, health, education, and recreation. Adam would still possess rights over the decision to marry and to have children. Of course, I could contest the order and file for these two additional rights, but to prohibit Adam from ever getting married or becoming a father was moot. These were a mother's dreams that would never be.

Let me explain.

Adam does not develop social relationships; it would be highly doubtful that he would ever develop a relationship that would evolve to the point of marriage. He just would not have that desire or understanding—not that any of us ever really do understand what we are signing on for when we say "I do," right? Should anyone want to marry Adam, it would be solely in a caretaker role, and the money he receives from SSI barely supports one person for a month. However, considering the changing politics of the day, I, a political person, found the hypocrisy of this to be most disturbing. Here is my son, who was just about to be declared legally incompetent, being given more rights by the state of California than a same-sex couple who wanted to get married and have children. I found something fundamentally wrong with this. Really disturbing. Inconsistent. Ridiculous. And because I can easily go off on a tangent, I pondered whether I should make a point of this—especially having prescient foresight, Proposition 8 was passed a mere three years later. I could have tumbled down a deep rabbit hole on this issue.

Fortunately, Josh's question "Do you think this would really matter to Adam?" brought me back into reasonableness; I accepted the limited conservatorship and signed the papers, which would be presented in court within the next ten days. The next Wednesday, we went to court. Adam, me, and our lawyer, Philip Gold.

Silver, Gold and Autism entered the courtroom of the Honorable Judge Sheila Honor (not kidding, that is her name) and were number 23 on the docket. Adam insisted that we should be number 18—after all, "July 18, 2005—Adam 18—*yes!*" I brought along books, pens, pencils, and paper to keep Adam occupied until our case was called. They were all conservatorship hearings and moved along quickly. It was the last formality of the process. All that was required was the judge's stamp of approval. When number 18 was called, Adam stood up. "Eighteen—*yes!*" Who says that people with autism don't pay attention? After another long twenty-minutes, number 23 was called.

As we walked through the little swinging doors that separate the gallery from the well and approached the podium, I flashed back to the only other time in my life that I had gone to court, which was when Adam's dad and I had to appear in front of a judge to publicly dissolve our marriage, making vows of divorce with the same convictions as when we united.

"Do you, Adam's dad, solemnly swear that this marriage has dissolved into a state of irreconcilable differences?"

"I do," Adam's dad had replied.

Oh, the dramatic irony of that two-word marriage vow.

The Honorable Judge Honor loomed above us at her imposing desk, looking larger than life, and Adam and I stood at the podium, me feeling like a cartoon Bugs Bunny being sentenced to hell. Judge Honor did not look up—or down—not at nor on us. She was flipping through the papers, making sure the *Is* were dotted and the *Ts* were crossed, ensuring that all the boxes were duly checked and all the signatures notarized. We waited quietly at the podium wondering if Adam or I would be interviewed. Attached to the little podium where we stood was a silver microphone. I had been so busy keeping Adam busy, that I could not tell you if any of the twenty-two cases that had proceeded us had spoken into it, but Adam spotted it right way.

Adam knows microphones.

Adam knows Dumbo.

Adam knows Timothy Mouse.

Adam knows Ringling Brothers' circus.

"Ladies and gentlemen! Boys and girls! Welcome to the greatest show on earth!"

The Honorable Judge Honor finally looked down at us from her towering desk, up there in the courtroom sky.

"Hello, Your Honor. Meet my son, Adam. He calls it like he sees it."

A slight grin crossed her lips. She closed the packet and stamped "APPROVED."

I speak English and I speak Adam. I do not doubt for a second that of all the memorized words and phrases churning around in that mysterious brain of his, Adam selected *exactly* what he thought of this entire process. Regardless, he would never have to worry that he would not be cared for in the best of all possible ways. More important than the signatures on the papers and the sounding of the gavel is the love in my heart.

Now, I not only had the joy of being his mom, I also had the privilege of being his conservator.

*Twelve years later, I have yet to decode what "pizza snake" means. He says it every time we see each other. I do promise you that I have never fed it to him.

ADDENDUM

(Please do not read if you easily take political offense.)

In 2008, three years later, Adam told me that he wanted to vote in the upcoming presidential election. I do not know who, what, where, from whom he learned about this, but he wanted to vote for Barack Obama. Now I could have made up some phony ballot and pretended that we were voting, but I am mandated by the laws of conservatorship to ensure that I best represent Adam in what he wants, so we scheduled a private visit with the Honorable Judge Honor to see what needed to be done to restore Adam's right to vote. Because he had been declared legally incompetent, I did not know whether this was a possibility. But because Prop 8 was also on the 2008 ballot, I felt I had a rational argument on his behalf—if he has the right to marry, he deserves the right to vote.

We went into Judge Honor's chambers where she welcomed us, recalling the story of "the greatest show on earth." I explained to her the purpose of our petition and sought her approval of reversing the stipulation, which would restore Adam's right to vote. I brought two pieces of evidence with me that might also work in Adam's favor: the first was his notice to register for the military with selected services and the second was a recent summons for jury duty. Someone in the government still saw Adam as an eligible person. Or at least their electronic filing system did. Judge Honor explained that she needed to hear the request directly from Adam.

"Hello, Adam, I understand that you want to vote in the upcoming election."

"Obama 08—we can't wait."

I sat there in silence. I swear, I did not teach him that. I had been a Hillary supporter.

"Adam, why do you want to vote for Mr. Obama?"

"The people."

Again, I swear, I did not prompt him at all. I had no idea where he learned this.

Judge Honor turned to me. "What I have to do here is render if Adam is capable of making a reasonable decision on his own."

Not knowing her personal politics, I know that I put Adam's chances for approval at risk as I considered my response. But the truth is the truth is the truth.

"Your Honor, if you will excuse me for begging the question," I began, "but if the criteria is based upon the ability to make a reasonable decision, what would you say about all the people currently supporting Sarah Palin?" I was wearing my poker face.

She looked at me. She looked at Adam. And then for the second time in our lives, the Honorable Judge Honor stamped "APPROVED."

Adam voted for the first time in the 2008 election. And again in 2012. And in November 2016. And in the most recent mid-term elections. He is looking forward to 2020.

CHAPTER 14

Boys' Club House

How many times have we, as parents, thought, *Ah! When will this be over?* Carpools, meetings, homework, soccer practice, homework—no, we are not having McDonald's"—we all know the drill. Yet as much as we as parents cannot wait for our kids to grow up, the truth is that what we really want is for time to slow down. And just like every normal mom raising a normal child, too often I wished time away. "*Oh, if only to go out without packing a diaper bag. Oh, I cannot wait until they can talk and end all this whining (as if that ever happens!). Oh, only two more years until they start school, then I will go on a diet and start running again.*" You know these thoughts, the ones we whisper to ourselves as we are packing school lunches at five thirty in the morning, the ones that are followed by "I am so tired. Will I ever not feel tired again?"

And then we blink and before we know it, they have grown up.

They get into the car for their first solo drive away from home. We hold our breath until we hear that car pull back in the driveway.

He poses for pictures with his beautiful prom date, looking so handsome in his tux.

She walks across the stage to receive her graduation diploma.

And then the absolute worst happens, and you cannot believe that you ever wished the years away. The day comes when your child goes away to college. It is only then that we realize our foolishness, and we wonder if we paid enough attention, if we gave them enough guidance, will they take our advice with them and use it to navigate life on their own? In 2004, there was nothing as simultaneously gratifying and fearful as moving Josh into his new address at California State University San Francisco—Mary Ward Hall, number 610.

It was the second week of August 2004, when we packed up the car with his clothes and all the new things we had bought at Bed, Bath, and Beyond to outfit his dorm room. Josh, Adam and I drove the 450 miles up Interstate 5 to San Francisco State where we were greeted by the seasoned RAs, the excited freshmen class and the other anxious parents struggling to let go. As if having his mom gush all over him wasn't embarrassing enough, Josh did his best to ignore his strangely autistic brother, who was making funny noises and wanting to strip down to his underwear and climb into his brother's dorm room bed.

My good friend and mentor, Robyn, who had done this three times before me, had warned me that the tension between parent and child as he takes off for college must have reached a peak where you are ready to drop kick your son into his new room. She was right. My freshman tolerated us just long enough to share a snack in the dining hall, where in my nervous anxiety over separating from Josh and hypervigilance over Adam, I proceeded to spill hot coffee all over myself. Who knows, maybe I subconsciously planned for this to happen because burning my lap with steaming-hot coffee gave me the excuse I needed to break down and cry. With one final hug where I hung on too long, Adam and I waved goodbye and drove away, leaving Josh to start his new life. Oh, how fast the years had flown.

I missed him as soon as I drove away from the cul-de-sac in front of the dorm and while Adam listened to his Disney songs, looking up every so often to check on me, I cried the entire 450-mile drive home.

It is good to "speak Adam."

"Mommy, no crying. Did I ever tell you how lucky you are? Can you feel the love tonight?"

In 2005, when Adam turned eighteen, besides becoming conserved, it meant that he had reached the end of his educational years in a formal classroom and would begin his transition program. At twenty-two, he would formally graduate from his education. At last I knew *not* to wish this time away.

The year 2009 would be the last year of school for Adam. For nineteen years he had been riding the little yellow Laidlaw school bus to and from school.

The spring before, we had returned to San Francisco State to see Josh receive his bachelor's degree. Even his dad and Mandy had flown in for this event.

What did Adam understand about graduation? Sure, he'd participated in ceremonies as he moved from preschool to elementary to middle and high school, but did he, or any of us for that matter, have any idea of what his life would look like once he turned twenty-two? As hard as his transition team had worked to prepare Adam for his next chapter in life, I was the one who needed the support. As June 18 drew near, Adam started saying, "Adam graduation. Joshie dorms—Adam dorms."

What did he say?

"Adam graduation. Joshie dorms—Adam dorms."

Taking out my "Adam decoder," this made perfect sense. Adam remembered that when Josh had graduated from high school, he had seen his big brother packing up and moving into the college dorms. And in Adam World, since he was graduating from his transition program, the time had come for him to move into the dorms as well. So many questions arose with this request—or demand—as the case may be. Most interestingly was the understanding that Adam did not see himself as any different from his brother. I had dedicated myself so completely that Adam would have the same life experiences as Josh: Josh played soccer and baseball; Adam played soccer and baseball. Josh went to summer camp; Adam went to summer camp. Josh moved into the dorms—well, you know the rest. In the timeline of life, Adam was ready to move out on his own. It took me three more years to adjust to this reality.

There were several reasons that moving into his own dorm was completely appropriate for Adam. First and foremost, he was turning twenty-two, would be exiting the transition program at Orange Coast College, and moving into the real world. He was set up with a job coach and would be entering the work force. Secondly, he was asking for this—he saw his brother moving on after high school, and he knew that this was the rightful passage into adulthood. Every Chanukah, Adam asks for only three things: the next *NOW* CD, a calendar for the new year, in which he fills every date he had ever memorized, and whenever we go out to eat, it is always *grilled cheese, french fries, and lemonade,* which in Adam speak *is* one inseparable menu item. So should he ask for something else, I need to pay attention. Finally, and this is the dark secret I do not want to share, Adam had become more and more aggressive, and I had become the object of his fists. Adam was taller, heavier, and stronger than me, and I was not able to deflect him quickly enough or with enough strength to physically protect myself. So yes, the incidents of my being pushed to the floor, attacked in the garage, being grabbed while driving were increasing, and I had to accept that I needed help. Because Adam does not have the verbal ability to sit down and have a rational conversation over a cup of coffee, he must find other ways to let us know what he is feeling. Frustrated? *Yes!* Angry? *Yes!* Confused? *Yes!* Disappointed? Perhaps. The list of emotions goes on and on. The only word Adam could come up with to explain what might be coming or what just happened was "*Volcano!*" which literally explains it all.

This was the secret that I had kept so deeply hidden. I did not want anyone to know that I was unable to handle my son 100 percent of the time. I had always taken the position that regardless of how hard situations felt to me, it had to be even worse for Adam. I could never be sure what would set him off, when it might happen and most frustratingly, why he would "Volcano!" It wasn't a secret in school; the mystery of Adam has always been the when, the where, and the why of what makes him explode. The good news was that his outbursts would last no more than twenty to thirty seconds. The bad news was that Adam could do a lot of damage in those twenty to thirty seconds. I had taken self-defense classes and knew how to get behind Adam to divert the physical charge, *if* I heard it or saw it coming. Most times, he would escalate from 0 to 150 in a matter of moments with no indication that the volcano was about to erupt. Over the years his teachers and I documented everything we could, trying to understand his pattern or the triggers. Nothing. To look at Adam in these moments, it is easy to see he is gone, lost, somewhere in the autistic brain. His eyes are glazed, he does not focus, he is like a wild animal ready to pounce. His need to hit, throw, kick, or bite is not directed purposefully toward any person. He does not distinguish between a wall, a chair, or me.

Adam and I had been on our own since 2004, and outside our school hours, we were together all the time. Part of the deeply held secret was that I was tired, worn out, and emotionally drained. One of the best parts of having a son like Adam is that his needs require that I be the best mom I can be, 100 percent of the time, but this level of parenting takes its toll. I live in hypervigilance, making sure that I know where he is at all times, doing my best to stay five steps ahead of his impulses. Just keeping him grounded requires that I not fade out even for a moment. And it was not just the meltdowns that wore me out. I had not known life without the "Adam factor" for twenty-two years. The need to weigh in and continuously evaluate "Can Adam handle this new restaurant, going to the Honda Center to see Disney on Ice, taking a different route when I drove somewhere?" and the expansion of this list goes on and on and on. I was tired, very, very tired. But still we kept going—making the best of our lives as mother and son.

There was this one afternoon when Adam and I had driven up to LA to walk around the Venice canals and explore the boardwalk. It was a beautiful June afternoon, and we enjoyed walking up and down the beach watching the waves and the sunset. To my horror, when we got back to the car which we parked at the local library, the parking lot had been chained off. There was no way for me to get my car out of the lot. Had it been today rather than 2007, I would have simply called an uber and come back the next day to retrieve my car. There were five cars who had been unwittingly locked in. Through a series of phone calls to the LAPD and the Auto Club, begging, pleading and then finally playing the "I have a son with a severe disability" card (which I hate doing), we were able to get someone to come down and unlock the chains so that the five trapped cars could quietly drive off. Adam held it together well, and since the Las Vegas incident, I knew to bring his meds along with us. Nearly three hours later, we arrived home, tired, hungry, and most significantly, after seven, which meant that we had missed *Jeopardy!* As soon as we got the car into the garage, Adam hurled himself at me, pushing me to the ground. And then…and then…although I thought I had hidden it well, he found the hammer and rushed toward me. I yelled, using my most loud and ferocious yell, and it brought him back into reality. People in our neighborhood had been out for an evening walk as the commotion began, and they stood at the end of the driveway watching this scene play out. No one offered to help or intervene. They just stood there staring at the middle-aged mom on the floor of the garage struggling to stand up and get the hammer away from her charging son. It's not that they just stood there doing nothing that upset me; it was that look on their faces, the looks of disgust and judgement that seer us. They judged him and me, creating their own stories of what was going on. I captured Adam in a bear hug and got the hammer out of his hand, and then I began to sob. The stress of it all broke me down. And as much as I love my son, it was this incident that convinced me that I could no longer care for him on my own; I needed help, my own safety was at risk, and I needed to rest. Although I felt like a failure as a mom and was ashamed to admit that I could no longer do this on my own, I was ready to accept that Adam needed to move into his "dorm." I rationalized this decision by looking at the big picture, telling myself that *"someday I will no longer be here, and it is important that Adam be set up in a life of his own,"* but my level of grief at what felt like yet another loss, was immense. I was mourning yet another rite of passage to life as I knew it. And as always, I had to ask myself Josh's question: "Does this matter to Adam?" Yes, this time it does—this is better for Adam—and for me.

Is it a *mom thing* that we love our children so deeply? That we would do anything to protect them from the evil, outside world? How? Where? Would I ever find a place where I could trust the well-being and safety of my son to others? I was sick with fear and dread as we began looking for the perfect "dorm" (if such a thing existed) for Adam. My rational brain told me that it was time for my son to live independently. My emotional brain could not grasp the reality. I desperately wanted to turn the clock back in time to when Adam was young enough and little enough to be able to protect him, but I had to let him go. Soon he would be twenty-five years old; it was time for Adam to be live independently.

Like all things having to do with Adam, our first step began with the Regional Center. Our wonderful caseworker, Nikki, was 100 percent supportive of this decision for all the right reasons, and to help me come to terms with this choice, she shared story after story (anonymously of course) of clients whose parents had not been able let go of their child, and who now, in their fifties and even sixties, were not only at a loss on how to function independently; they were now alone in the world. Nikki initiated the process on our behalf, and we began the search for "Boys' Club House," a.k.a. "Adam's Dorm." And like all things having to do with Adam, step 2 was that he would be assessed and tested to determine what "level house" would be best for him.

Group Home levels are determined by how much supervision a client—now legally called a consumer—requires. While Adam is perfectly able to care for his personal needs—bathroom, shower, hygiene, grooming, dressing himself—even choosing clothes that match nicely—feeding himself, and sleeping all through the night, his communication skills and behaviors demand close attention. In general, he is compliant and seeks permission to engage in an activity or leave the house, which legally, he is *never* supposed do alone, but in a matter of seconds, he can completely disappear, wander off somewhere, go on a "mission" with such stealth, that it is only when we notice the absence of his droning that we think to ask "Where has he gone?" It is this need for hypervigilance that landed him on the list for a 4-I Home—the highest level of supervision of a 2:1 consumer-caretaker ratio. In looking over the checklist for the placement recommendation forms, I wanted to argue that my son was more capable and did not require *that much supervision*" and could be more independent. Just because I had always micromanaged his life didn't mean that it had to continue this way, right? Nikki asked me to come outside the conference room for a private chat.

"Will you please be quiet!" she whispered through one side of her mouth, all the while smiling so that the rest of the team, who could see us through the glass windows, could not sense her tension.

"Why?" I challenged. "Adam is so much more capable than this report suggests."

"Yes, this may be true. But, Sheila, parents clamor and fight to have their children placed in a 4-I house. They are the *best* homes, with the *best* caretakers, and he will receive the *most* attention. Now shut up and get out of your own way."

She opened the door and we went back into the room. That is why Regional Center provides a caseworker for people like me because I need someone to constantly remind me that I do not know everything. And in this case, I did not know anything. I took the directive, shut up, and let her do her job.

Once all agreed upon and signed the paperwork for Adam to move into a 4-I group home, I was given a list of four homes that had "beds available" and was invited to visit them all, interview the home owners and house managers, check out the other consumers who lived there and then decide which of the houses would be best for Adam. Time was not an issue, with the exception that there are more consumers seeking placement than there are beds available, I gave myself four months to plan and get Adam moved into his new digs. As if this was going to be easy. As if I could really let him go. The goal was that he would be in his own home for the start of the 2007 school year. We targeted mid-August for the move in date.

At the beginning of my second year of college, I, the awkward girl who never fit in anywhere, was persuaded by my best friend to join her in sorority rush. I had no more business pledging a sorority than I did going out for the Miss America pageant, but I joined her for three days of teas and parties and being oh so charming. As it happened, the Regional Center was hosting an open-house event at available group homes, so one afternoon in early June, I visited the four available options. It felt like I was back in sorority rush, meeting people, eating more than my share of the snacks provided at each home to dissuade my stress, checking out the rooms, the backyards, and the activity calendars, and once again hoping that one of the homes would "pick me." As if I was the one who would be accepted or blackballed as I had experienced so many years ago. I learned much at those open houses, listening to my gut reaction, observing the cleanliness of the home, and walking around the neighborhoods. I wondered if neighbors had protested when a group home for adults with disabilities moved onto their street. Memories of parents with 'normal kids' picketing schools when "those kids" were mainstreamed into classrooms after the passage of PL94-142 began to obsess my thoughts. Will Adam be safe here? Will they care for him? Will he be happy? I was overwhelmed with fear and anxiety, my head spun, and I did not think I could go through with this plan. I was scared even though there was nothing, absolutely nothing I observed that gave any impression other than these were good, clean homes who provided a valuable and needed service for members of society who deserved to live full and productive lives. Still, I hated them all—hated all this—and I retreated into a state of denial once more.

By mid-July, I had recouped, found what I believed would be a great place, and began preparing Adam for his new life in the "dorms." The transition began by having him visit Boys' Club House for dinner, then for a few hours after school, then for lunch and dinner so that with each visit, he became more and more comfortable with the environment. He would have a private bedroom, and in week three, we slowly began to take his personal belongings with us and left them there along with some clothes, toys, books, and wall hangings. By the last week in August, his new room at Boys' Club House looked like the one he was leaving behind. Just as I had done with Josh as he was preparing to go away to college, Adam and I went shopping at Bed, Bath, and Beyond, and he picked out a bedspread, blankets, sheets, towels, a lamp—all the necessities for a dorm room. By the day he was *for real* moving in, we had very little to carry over with us. And all too soon, that day came.

I had a pit in my stomach that I hadn't felt since the day of my mother's death. I could not eat. I could not sleep. I felt hollow and empty inside. You would think that he was moving to the other side of the world. Boys' Club House was less than five miles away. I could visit there every day, anytime, day or night. He could come spend as much time with me at home as he wanted, any time, day or night. But to paraphrase Neil Armstrong, this was one small step for Adam, one giant step for Adam's mom.

August 27 was set as the move-in date. The night before I sat with Adam in his room, his last night officially living with me, my last night of motherhood, or so it seemed. We kept everything routinely normal, *Jeopardy!* at seven, shower, PJs, brush teeth, into bed by eight. Routine. Our routine. So why was my stomach such a mess? At 2:00 p.m., on Wednesday, we went over to Boys' Club House, not for a visit but to stay. Two suitcases of clothes, we put them into his new chest of drawers and hung-up shirts in the closet. We made it a celebration—cake, balloons, and a "Welcome Adam" sign for his bedroom door. Adam and I were in his room, hanging up the last of the family pictures he had chosen to hang on his walls, when he sat down on his bed scanning his new surroundings.

"Mommy?" he asked. "Adam's books?"

"Right here on your bookcase," I replied.

"Adam's computer?"

"Over there on the desk."

"Adam's TV?"

"On top of your bookcase."

He paused. He looked around the room. "Magic?"

"No, honey, Magic"—our 110-pound black lab—"will stay at Mom's place."

Another pause. He looked around the room. "Mommy?"

"I will be at Cambridge House" (name of the street we lived on).

Another pause. He looked around the room. He pondered. Silence. And then he said, "See ya later! Bye-bye, Mom."

And that was that.

I had been dismissed.

Just goes to show you—sometimes you do things right.

Adam's adjustment to living in a group home was remarkable in that there was no adjustment time at all. He just started living there, happily, enjoying his independent life. I wish I could say that the adjustment was as easy for me. The reactions from those around me affected me in several ways. There were those who told me how brave and courageous I was to let him move to a group home. And to them I would confess how guilty and scared I felt—I was not brave or courageous at all. And there were those who criticized me for abandoning my son, to whom I would say "You have no idea what I was living with—it was time for him to be on his own." And then there were those who congratulated me on having prepared Adam so well for this huge change in his life, but I could not take any credit for this. Adam was ready to move on and it all came from within him. The biggest lesson I learned from this was to listen and follow Adam's lead. I learned to trust him, my wise and brilliant son. He continues to amaze me in the most awesome ways.

On Children
Kahlil Gibran

Your children are not your children.
They are the sons and daughters of Life's longing for itself.
They come through you but not from you,
And though they are with you, yet they belong not to you.
You may give them your love but not your thoughts.
For they have their own thoughts.
You may house their bodies but not their souls,
For their souls dwell in the house of
tomorrow, which you cannot visit,
not even in your dreams.
You may strive to be like them, but seek not to make them like you.
For life goes not backward nor tarries with yesterday.
You are the bows from which your children
as living arrows are sent forth.
The archer sees the mark upon the path of the infinite, and He
bends you with His might that His arrows may go swift and far.
Let your bending in the archer's hand be for gladness;
For even as he loves the arrow that flies, so
He loves also the bow that is stable.

From *The Prophet*

CHAPTER 15

La Traviata

From the time he began with the County Autism Program, it took three years for Adam to start talking again. And apparently, we were the last to know that at school he had been talking for quite some time. Surprise!

Our family and friends had stopped inviting us over; they were just too uncomfortable with either us or Adam or having to deal with the reality that they had a grandchild, nephew, or cousin with severe autism. Even though we arrived with two cars, one to stay and the other to leave when Adam had maxed out, we were just not welcomed anymore. But for those who worked with Adam, Mr. Adorable won their hearts, especially his teachers and classroom aides. Two of the aides begged us to let them come over and babysit him on the weekends. Really? Someone wants to be with Adam? Adam's favorite was Ms. Brenda, a young woman so full of energy and life who could play with Adam for hours. An angel. One of their favorite games, like most six-year-olds, was tickle. Ms. Brenda could get Adam into a rollicking laugh, full of vibrant joy, and all of us would laugh along with him. It was contagious in the best of all possible ways. And then…and then…one Saturday evening during a game of tickle, Ms. Brenda was prompting, "What do you say, Adam, what do you say?"

"I love you."

And there it was, spoken as clear as day.

Adam's dad, Josh and I shut up in amazement. We stared at Adam. We stared at Ms. Brenda. We stared at each other. In disbelief. In shock. In amazement.

"What's the matter?" asked Ms. Brenda, mirroring the expressions on our faces. "Is something wrong?

Did he just say "I love you"?

"Of course, he did," she answered nonchalantly, "he talks all the time. You don't know this?"

I could have been imagining it, but had Adam had the words, I am certain he would have said, "Oh shit—my cover is blown."

Day after day, week after week, month after month, we sat at that same old Tiny Tots table working with Adam on the language and communication exercises that we had been trained to do. Nothing. Silence. Direct and redirect. Eye contact. M&Ms. Prompting.

And all we needed to do was tickle him into submission!

It was a joyful moment in our home.

Ha, Adam! We gotchor number! We gotchor number!

I speak English. I speak Spanish. I speak Hebrew. And I speak Adam.

Like the miraculous moment when Helen Keller first said *water*, Adam's world began to have meaning to us. He always knew what he was saying—writing. FHE, FHE—we finally figured it out—the three letters on the case of his favorite Richard Scary video: "Family Home Entertainment." All over the walls, on the carpet, in the car. FHE—at last we knew. There was no limit to the words coming out of him. To the average ear, his voice sounded monotone, unintelligible, slurred gibberish. To us, we were learning to speak and read Adam. Who knew what was locked up in there after so many years of input? Had he really been paying attention…to everything? Yes, his words sounded jumbled, confused, and disconnected, but he was speaking "Adam," and he had no doubts about what he was saying. It was up to us to learn this new language.

Just as Adam loved his books, he also loved to watch *Jeopardy!* At 7:00 p.m. Monday through Friday, Alex Trebeck was in our living room. Adam was transfixed. We recorded the episodes so that he could watch them over and over again. Which he loved to do. Which is why we had to be near a television at 7:00 p.m. every Monday through Friday. Remember that scene in *Rainman,* "*Jeopardy*—four o'clock." We learned that this does not only exist in a screenplay. Long before the DVR, Adam would watch each episode of *Jeopardy* over and over again via the now obsolete VCR. Rewind was his best friend. We blew through four or five VCRs a year due to his need to rewind, rewind, rewind the videos. Years later when Mandy bought Disney Scene It, Adam, the one-man team, easily out played the rest of us because he knew every frame of every Disney cartoon and movie ever made. We also realized that not only had he been paying attention to everything, he had also memorized everything about whatever he was watching—the year of production, the names in the credits, the colors of every character's clothing along with the entire script. Back to *Rainman*—"Who's on First." Hmm, the benefits of repetition. He could recite it all.

So back to *Jeopardy!* One night we were sitting on the couch, 7:00 p.m., it was a Wednesday night, February 1995, and Adam was seven years old. The category was geography for $400.

Alex read the clue: *This Canadian province lies between Alberta and Manitoba.*

Adam answers, "What is Saskatchewan?"

This was not a repeat episode. It was the College Tournament of Champions Semifinals.

Yet another stunning moment in our home. We were the ones who were stunned. We stared at Adam. We stared at Alex Trebeck. We stared at each other. In disbelief. In shock. In amazement. How *could* he know that? How could he know *that?* The only one not surprised was Adam. I could have been imagining it, but had Adam had the words, I am certain he would have said, "What is the matter with you idiots—everybody knows that." We then began to understand how ridiculous it was for us to wonder what Adam knew or didn't know; there is so much information in him! He had been memorizing foreign language dictionaries for years and would go to bed with the letter *S* encyclopedia instead of soft, furry stuffed animals. It is our job to pay attention to what comes out of him and learn to decipher it. The symbol for the Autism Society is a puzzle piece. I would have made it a Rubik's cube.

Which is exactly why I should not have been surprised at all when in 2010 Adam came home one day and said, "Mommy, I want *La Traviata*."

"*La Traviata*, Adam?" I said, making sure I had heard him correctly. "*La Traviata?*"

"LA Opera"—pronounced "La," as in *La Traviata*—"yes!"

In Adam speak that means, "I want us to go to the opera, Mom. LA Opera is performing *La Traviata* and I want you to take me. Make it happen." Of course, Adam knows about opera. He knows about opera because Adam has watched the cartoon *Willy the Operatic Whale Who Wanted to Sing at the MET* ten thousand times. If Adam had the words, he would have said, "What the heck is the matter with you, Mom, that you would doubt that I am not cultured enough to know about the opera? After all, you took me to see Josh's shows for every performance and I memorized Shakespeare. Give me a break." Or something like. But being a minimalist like Hemingway, he simply says, "LA Opera—yes!" and I fill in the commentary. "LA Opera—yes!" and then Adam began to sing the same aria that Willy had sung at his brilliant audition for the Empresario from *Willy the Operatic Whale Who Wanted to Sing at the Met*—"Figaro, Figaro, Figaro" (http://www.cornel1801.com/disney/Make-Mine-Music-1946/film9.html 5:20).

See why it can be so much fun having someone with autism in your life? It's like learning to read a tornado. Those crazy scientists who chase the tornado and throw those communication sensor balls into its vortex, they can figure out the inside thoughts of the tornado; that's what it is like learning to read Adam. Who knows what you will learn. It's darn fascinating!

Sure enough, I googled LA Opera, and in June, they were going to be performing La Traviata to the pop of $250 a ticket. Oh, La Opera, why must you be so expensive? "Figaro, Figaro, Figaro. LA Opera—*yes*!" We reached a compromise, and instead of going to LA Opera, which I would have loved for us to do but could not afford, we started attending the Saturday morning *Live from the MET* HD broadcasts at our local AMC, and they are wonderful. Again, there are parts of going to these performances with Adam that baffle me, even after all these years. Here is this young man who cannot sit at a table in a restaurant for one minute longer after he has finished his grilled cheese, French fries, lemonade, "*Done!*" yet he is captivated for over four hours while we attend *Live from the MET*. The high definition is so intimate, you can almost feel the spittle coming from the performers' mouths and count their nose hairs. And because most operas are sung in Italian or German, Adam loves reading the English subtitles. In addition to the amazing performers, the music, the spectacle and the beautiful costumes, the opera is also part of Adam's literacy project! At $25 a ticket this is a much more affordable option for us, even though, snob that I am, I do worry about the sanctity and preservation of live theater. However, when the camera pans the filled-to-capacity Lincoln Center, I realize that I have been worrying over nothing. The broadcasts begin at 9:55 a.m. PST, and it is well past 1:00 p.m. when we leave the movie theater. I love the experience of going to the opera with Adam. For all the challenges of autism, he asks for so little. And if going to the opera makes him happy, to the opera we will go.

Some Saturday mornings, Adam must decide if he wants to go to baseball practice or to LA Opera. I love it that he has these choices and that he enjoys so many things. Another entertainment that

Adam enjoys is going to a drumming circle. On a recent Saturday morning, Adam decided to go to baseball practice but told me, "Mommy—five o'clock—drumming circle la opera." I scratched my head. What did he want to do? "Mommy—five o'clock—drumming circle la opera." Okay, like so many times before, I will figure it out. I just went for the obvious. Let's take some cardboard boxes and some wooden spoons, and at five o'clock, we will have our own concert in the park, "Drumming Circle LA Opera."

It was a beautiful fall evening in Long Beach, and with our cardboard boxes and wooden spoons, we drove to Belmont Park where we could watch the sunset as we had our two-person drumming circle. There were many families and couples of all ethnic backgrounds enjoying a peaceful picnic in the park. Across the harbor was the Queen Mary, and as the sky changed from blue to violet to yellow and orange, Adam began to play his drum. He sang "Puff the Magic Dragon" and "Zippidy Doo-Dah" all to the perfect rhythm of our improvised drums. We played for a while and sang a few more songs and then he said, "Mom, *Willy the Operatic Whale Who Wanted to Sing at the MET.*" Wonderful! We will be serenaded with a rousing rendition of "Figaro, Figaro, Figaro."

Now, what I did not know, but what Adam knew from having memorized the entire cartoon, was that in this 1946 Disney film called *Make Mine Music,* Willy the Whale sang a number of songs in addition to *The Marriage of Figaro.* Back in 1946, there was no concern called political correctness and just like back in those more innocent days—or days of ignorance, you decide—Adam simply wanted to sing one of the songs from *Willy the Operatic Whale Who Wanted to Sing at the MET.* Hmmm…it wasn't "Figaro, Figaro, Figaro." In his loudest, most confident, operatic imitation of good ol' Willy, Adam began to sing (http://www.cornel1801.com/disney/Make-Mine-Music-1946/film9.html 3:18).

Mammy's little baby loves short'nin', short'nin',
Mammy's little baby loves short'nin' bread.

Put on de skillet, put on de lead,
Mammy's gonna make a little short'nin' bread.
Dat aint all she's gonna do,
Mammy's gonna make a little coffee too.

All eyes in Belmont Park turned our way. Especially those belonging to our black American neighbors who were picnicking near us.

Three little darkies lying in bed
Two was sick an' the other 'most dead.
Send for the doctor, the doctor said,
"Feed dose darkies on short'nin' bread!"

"Adam," I shouted before he got too far into that first verse. "*Stop!*"

Oh my god—all he wanted to do have an opera drumming circle, and here we had offended about twenty people who just wanted to enjoy a quiet evening in Belmont Park. What to do, what to do?

Like Willy the Whale, Adam was singing with great joy and self-expression. That was the day that I learned that if there are people in the world who become personally or politically offended by the purity of my son's song, I just cannot worry about that. That is for them to deal with. No hurt. No malice. Adam knows a freedom that political correctness can not suppress. Who am I to take away Adam's voice after he worked so hard to find it again?

So in my loudest, most confident, operatic imitation of good ol' Willy, I began to sing:

"Sorry, folks, no offense intended. He was singing *La Traviata*!"

CHAPTER 16

Take Me Out

We are very fortunate to live within ten minutes driving distance to Angel Stadium. It takes us longer to park the car and walk to our seats than it does to drive there. I cannot say that I was particularly fond of baseball or the Angels, but I had a mom who *loved* this team and who, for the last ten years of her life, had fantastic season tickets, traveled to Arizona for spring training and who, for a few years, was vice president of the Angels' Booster Club. She was also very lucky. Ne'er missing an opportunity to buy a raffle ticket, that woman won more Angel paraphernalia and tickets than anyone you could ever meet. And being generous, she gave us the extra tickets to go to the games.

For whatever reason, Adam loves going to Angel games. It does not make much sense. Always crowded with too many people, so much noise, yelling and screaming, inconvenient parking, the smells, sounds, and sensations of the stadium creates sensory overload for those of us who are neurotypical. But defying all we know about autism, Adam loves going to Angel games. Of course, we have our routines. We must sit in Section 424, we must have nachos with cheese, we must have lemon chill at the end of the fourth inning and we must sing "Take Me Out to the Ballgame" during the seventh inning stretch.

I am never sure if Adam is watching the same game I am, or if he is watching the game at all. But I will tell you this, he is 100 percent accurate when it comes to guessing the daily attendance when the options come up on the Jumbotron, he always predicts which animated cartoon figure will win the rounding of the bases, and in recent years, he knows to take his hat off when we sing the national anthem. This is one place that he is so comfortable that he can independently navigate himself from our seats to the men's bathrooms and back. We have been going for so many years that Jim, the stadium usher assigned to section 424, knows us by name, and secretly keeps an eye on Adam to make sure he comes and goes safely. I know that there are those who would and do criticize me for allowing Adam to venture off on his own, but the other side of the coin is that he deserves to experience moments of independence in his life without me or someone else hovering over him. At least to take a whiz, right?

Adam's absolute favorite night at Angel Stadium is Big Bang Friday. At the end of the game, all the stadium lights go out and they put on the biggest, brightest, most spectacular firework display. They out Disney Disneyland. The only fireworks that surpass Big Bang Friday is the extravaganza at Angel Stadium if they have a home game on the Fourth of July. There is such a cacophony of noise and music, and although Adam puts his hands over his ears, he is transfixed by the lights exploding in the sky. I love them too. And the games are even more special when Josh comes down and joins us. Oh my, the joy of sharing a brewski and a dog with my son at the baseball game (Adam has no interest in beer). Who knew that having adult children would be just so great!

Neither Adam nor I have any attachment to teams or players. Most of the time I have no idea who the Angels are playing, and honestly, since the 2002 World Series, I cannot name a team member on the roster. Okay—Albert Pujols and Mike Trout—Ha! I will tell you, however, that there is an excitement at Angel Stadium whenever they are playing the Yankees or the Red Sox. Loyalties hold fast, and it seems that every transplant to Southern California from the East Coast comes out for these games; in fact, I render that these fans outnumber those of us rooting for the home team. The tail gate parties are bigger, the noise louder, the language more colorful, and the rivalries hotter. I love going to these games. There was one game in July 2009 that was especially rousing. The score was tied at the bottom of the ninth, which meant we were going into overtime. This, however, was something that I had not explained to Adam, so that when the scoreboard went into the 10th inning, my son announced, "Baseball—nine innings—*done!*"

Oh no! Even I was caught up in the game and wanted to stay.

"Mommy—baseball, nine innings—*done!*"

He stood up to leave.

"Adam—sit down—more baseball."

"Nooooooo…more…baseball! *Done! Take me out!*"

I tried to negotiate with the promise of another Lemon Chill, but he was beginning to escalate, and so, as shared in an earlier chapter, I had to let the Wookie win. Damn it.

Now like everything else, where we park at the stadium is also part of our routine. I refuse to pay for preferred parking, but knowing how to time our arrival just right, we can usually find our way to park thirteen rows behind the cement barricade that separates general from preferred parking facing the two giant red hats that adorn the outside of the stadium at the center field entrance. But on this night, because the game was sold out to so many Bostonians, we ended up parking near the third base entrance. We never park there. So as you can imagine, Adam began the evening annoyed that we were not in our usual general parking area. Holding my frustration in, we walked down the ramps from section 424 and proceeded to our car, clearly the *only people* leaving the stadium during overtime of this exciting game. Or so we thought. As we neared our car, we encountered two very shit-faced fans, one Angels and one Red Sox, going at each other in the parking lot. They were so drunk, stumbling over one another, during what we first thought was a couple of buddies leaning on one another but quickly realized that we were witnessing a heated, drunken brawl. I took out my cell phone and dialed 911, if only to ensure that neither one of these assholes got into their cars and tried to drive. They could barely stand up for God's sake. I knew that the Anaheim Police Department patrolled Angel Stadium and would be there in less than a minute. To our shock, the man with the Red Sox hat pulled out a gun and pointed it at us. *At us.* Adam screamed, "Hospital—ambulance—jail!" Adam threw himself on the ground, hitting his head and continuing to scream, "Hospital—ambulance—jail!" The Angels' fan yelled, "Holy shit!" I threw myself on top of Adam, the Boston fan dropped  the gun to the ground, and then the Angels' fan then threw himself down on top of me. "Don't worry, lady—I gotcha covered," slurred the stinky, drunk Angels' fan. I remained motionless and Adam screamed, "Mommy off—Mommy off." The Red Sox fan tried to run just as the APD, honest to God, showed up on his horse. All in the dark parking lot of Angel Stadium. It happened so fast—but in slow motion—like an out-take in a Quentin Tarrentino movie. Just then, two rockets red glared into the sky, just like when we sing "The Star-Spangled Banner" at the top of the game, and the halo on the "Big A" lit up like a beacon letting all of Anaheim know the game was over. "Hell yeah," shouted the guy on top of me, "Angels take it!"

Who knows why we end up where we end up and why we ended up there? All I know is that I believe with all my heart that because of Adam's insistence that baseball ends at the end of nine innings, we might have helped save someone's life that night—or two, or four. "Hospital—ambulance—jail!" will forever be life-saving words in the Adam dictionary. He insisted that I "take me out," and so we did.

CHAPTER 17

Brothers' Day

Adam is actually a very simple guy and outside the demands of autism, he asks for very little. Where most children have lists and lists "what I want for Christmas or my birthday," Adam keeps things very simple. Every year for Chanukah, he asks for the same two items. The first is always the most recent *NOW* CD, which he never listens to, but he devotes himself to memorizing the songs on the CD by number, title and year. Oh, if only Steve Harvey or Ellen would host a game show called "Those Amazing Awe-Tistics," where the goal was to name every *NOW* song:

Steve Harvey: "What is song number 14 on *NOW* 22?"

Adam: "'Walk Away,' Kelly Clarkson."

He would beat out any contestant who ever played *Jeopardy!* and we would be very rich. No need to count cards like in *Rainman*, Adam memorizes everything.

The second item is always a calendar for the New Year. He used to be nonspecific; however, in recent years, he has told me the type of calendar he wants: 2017 was horses; 2018 was cats; 2019 was houses.

If I had my act more together, I would plan and order a calendar from Amazon.com (note to self—remember to do this for 2020) but alas, on the day before the first night of Chanukah, I have a scavenger hunt going from store to store until I find the right calendar. This year, against all my moral principles, Josh and I ended our search at Walmart where the closest thing we could find was a 2019 Thomas Kincaid Calendar of Churches. Since most of them were of small British houses of worship, we thought that this could suffice. Josh tried valiantly to persuade me to get the Bacon Lovers' Calendar instead, but I held out for Thomas Kincaid. After all, one cannot purchase a nonkosher calendar for Chanukah.

Once the calendar is unwrapped and the cellophane removed, Adam will spend the next two hours filling in every important date and holiday, month by month, hour by hour. He begins on January 1, "Happy New Year"; February, "Happy Valentine's Day"; March, "St. Patrick's Day" and "Mommy's Birthday" all the way through December, for which he already knows the first night of Chanukah (which changes every year—and I have no idea how he already knows except for I am sure that he had them memorized through 2350) and finally December 29, which is "Grandma Florrie Flowers." What this means is that on my mom's birthday we will go to the cemetery. He holds me to it twice a year, "Mother's Day and Grandma Florrie's Birthday—*yes!*" You get the drill.

He then moves onto the minor dates which include everyone's birthday with whom Adam has ever been in school: his teachers, teacher's aides, and even my former students whom he has met while coming with me to help build sets for my shows on the weekends. He writes their names onto the day and then their ages. Hey, Nick Welter, September 7—twenty years old—You make the calendar every year, buddy! Winnie, Adam's imaginary friend, was "born" in 2005, and her birthday, May 7, is always marked on the calendar. This year she turns fourteen.

The last dates to make it onto the calendars are the vacations Adam plans. March 2015—Adam and Josh Chicago. July 2017—Mommy and Adam Disney World. He's already planning to go to Hawaii for his thirty-third birthday. Unfortunately, none of these trips is in our budget, but Adam enjoys writing them on the calendar and then reminding us, and reminding us, and reminding us, and reminding us *ad infinitum* as part of his memorized tropes. We even have June 4, 11:30 a.m. lunch at Ruby's Diner because back in 1996, we had lunch at Ruby's on the Huntington Beach pier. Adam is the memory keeper.

It was back in December 2006, the day Adam was filling in his 2007 calendar, that he stopped suddenly and came over to ask me, "Mommy, Brothers' Day?"

"What, Honey?"

"May 9, Mother's Day. June 20, Father's Day. Brothers' Day?"

"I don't know, Sweetie. When do you want to have Brothers' Day?"

Adam stopped for a moment and returned to his calendar. He turned to July and on the twenty-fifth he wrote, "Josh, Adam, Brothers' Day."

I was fascinated. Once again, for all those who want to believe that people with autism do not feel emotions or connect with others, Adam had just created a new holiday!

I asked him, "What are you and Josh going to do on Brothers' Day?"

He thought for a minute and then replied, "Angel game."

Lordy, I thought, *please let the Angels be playing in Anaheim that day*. Sure enough, there was a 12:35 p.m. game against the Texas Rangers. Of course, Adam had the Angels' season completely memorized too.

"Okay, let's call Josh and tell him."

"Angel game, nachos, fourth inning lemon chill, seventh inning, "Take Me Out to the Ballgame," ninth inning—bye-bye, Angels."

Sure enough—seven months later when July arrived, Adam made Josh a "Happy Brothers' Day" card, and I took care of getting them the tickets in Section 424 for the game. Adam was very specific. I made arrangements to have "Happy Brothers' Day Adam and Josh" to be flashed on the Jumbotron. Kind of like in *Field of Dreams*!

Brothers' Day is now on the calendar every year on the fourth Sunday in July.

As Josh tells his friends, "Grab your brother, a beer and a dog and head on out to Angel Stadium."

Adam just wants to be sure that all the dates are listed—through 2350.

We compromised on the next 10!

July 24, 2016
July 23, 2017
July 22, 2018
July 28, 2019
July 26, 2020
July 25, 2021
July 24, 2022
July 23, 2023
July 28, 2024
July 27, 2025

"Grab your brother, a beer and a dog," and head on out to your nearest baseball stadium. Brothers' Day—it's great to celebrate your brother!

The Final Chapter—for Today

As I wrap up this memoir of these thirty years of parenting, there are so many things that I still wish for—some of them realistic but most of which are in the realm of the impossible. I hope that our story has given you some laughs and has helped you to understand a little bit more about the world of autism. Maybe, for as we now say, "If you've met one person with autism, you've met one person with autism." Most of all, I hope that our story leaves you with a little more acceptance and compassion for your own family or for others.

I have learned that laughing about all this is less painful than the anxiety that I experience daily. Sure, there are days when I feel upbeat and optimistic and see myself as a Polly Anna kind of a girl. But most days I struggle as Adam's mom, and I am at a loss at how to help him. I rarely feel safe—I have ended up in the hospital after being attacked by my son; I am constantly expected to provide the answers as to why my son turns into the Incredible Hulk. I wallow in sadness and despair more than I would like to admit, but my intention is not to invite you to my pity party. Conversely, I want our journey to inspire, motivate, and give you moments of hope and joy; living with autism is not easy—indeed there are moments of fear, stress and loss, but given the odds, there are far more moments—some remarkable and some even remarkably easy—when we are collectively embraced by good people who care about and love us.

In wrapping up our story (for now, for I am certain that by the end of this week, I will have another chapter or two to share), I want to be rigorously honest with you: this journey has been long, and it has been hard. And most times, I feel very alone. Having lived in a state of hypervigilance for all these many years, I have used up my lifetime supply of serotonin so I am on antidepressants, and to this I say, "God bless pharmaceuticals!" They help my son, and they help me. The world is safer for us all because we accept the help that is available. What I want to say is, I find tremendous love, joy, and gratitude in being Adam's mom, and that is what I want for all of us who care for *All the Adams in the World*.

If, in any of these chapters, our lives have come across as being easy or carefree, I assure you, they have not been. I have not meant to dismiss or marginalize what we families, who love someone on the autism spectrum, experience. In every situation, I am challenged to decide—will I stand strong and do all I can to support my son, or will I give into the depression and anxiety that make me want to park our car on the railroad tracks? I am grieved to say that yes, there are times when I feel hopelessly overwhelmed and can see no relief. But as my rabbi reminds me, the highest mitzvah is to save a life, and so, finding our way through whatever labyrinth we are in, I (once again) find my inner strength and navigate our way out. Even at 31, Adam still has meltdowns; he drones and makes funny noises and regardless of where we go to eat, he will only order grilled cheese, french fries, and lemonade. Just last Monday we went to Sea World, where they have a well-labeled "Grilled Cheese Concession Stand." Adam saw this and went ballistic when he learned that it is only open on the weekends. Surely, if the sign on the kiosk reads *Grilled Cheese*, it must be available. You do not want to know the scene that ensued—it was not pretty. And after I was able to get Adam calmed down and reassure the many onlookers who were staring at us with "The Look," I let myself secretly shed a few tears. "Mommy—no crying." Our roles are reversed. "Did I ever tell you how lucky you are?" It is in these moments when I feel most alone in the world. My head wants to travel down the rabbit hole of past hurts, abandonment, and despair. I do my best to hold it together, and as much as I want to crawl into that hole, the only thing I can do is make sure that Adam does not hurt himself or anyone else. Two minutes feels like two hours, and when Shamu Security comes running over, I feel embarrassed and lose all dignity begging them to "please get someone to open up the grilled cheese stand and make my son a sandwich."

They do not understand—how could they?

The day before we were at the Special Olympics Games at Point Loma University in San Diego. My head wants to wander to the bad neighborhood, pacing alone in the alleys of sorrow, me feeling isolated as the only single parent on our team. Adam has only me to cheer him on. And even though Josh describes my personality and love as being as large and enthusiastic as the entire family in *My Big Fat Greek Wedding*, I feel inadequate and ashamed that I am it—one mom in the stands cheering for her son. Because the circumstances of all these years have left me with major depression disorder, feeling sad is my natural tendency; I can easily forget to remember all that I have been writing to you. I forget that I can make the emotional choice to focus on what is going well. It is cold and overcast when we arrive at the track, but by the time the opening ceremonies begin, the sun is shining its glory over the Pacific Ocean. The Olympic theme song blares from the loud speakers and the athletes, along with their buddies, proudly march around the track. The parents sit in the stands cheering and waving signs. The Special Olympics Oath is pledged:

" Let me win, but if I cannot win, let me be brave in the attempt. "
(Motto of the Special Olympics)

Adam is signed up for three events; the first being the fifty-yard dash. He is seeded with other athletes who run at the same pace.

Actually—more of a saunter than a run! The gun goes off—six of his coaches stand along the inside track screaming for him, "*Run, Adam! Run!*" He starts in first, then falls to second, then third, and finishes in fourth place as the other athletes out run him. But as he crosses the finish line, the coaches rush to him and they all fall to the ground in joy! Adam ran the whole fifty-yards, and he stayed in his own lane. The parents in the stands jump up and down chanting "*Adam— Adam—Adam,*" hugging me and screaming "Did you see that? Did you see *that*? Sheila, he ran the whole way—he ran the whole way!" Head Coach Jenn sobs as the rest of her coaching team surrounds her. I am pulled back into reality. I am not alone. WE—are not alone. Our lives are filled with loving, supportive people who care and understand. One small step for man—one huge race for Adam!

He happily accepts his fourth-place white ribbon. Later that day, Adam won a bronze medal in the softball throw and a gold in the standing broad jump. The fact that he was the only participant in his age bracket in that event did not deter the enthusiasm of the medal presentation in the least!

It really doesn't matter that twenty-four hours later, this victorious athlete will be freaking out over a grilled cheese sandwich at Sea World. We got through it. And we will get through it again.

What matters is that in this world of special needs, a world that ebbs and flows with joy and stress, none of us are alone. Even my crazy, depressed head knows this.

I want to cradle the faces of parents whose children are newly diagnosed. I want to hold them close and look into their eyes. I want to say, "Do not be afraid. You are about to embark upon an amazing journey that is going to be filled with experiences and people that you cannot even begin to imagine. Yes, it is scary. And yes, there are times when you will feel anxious and fearful and alone. We all do. You will also be angry and filled with so much resentment that you too will want to 'Volcano!' And you will. But, my darlings, please remember this—you are being given the opportunity to live an extraordinary life. Remember to stand back and watch it sometimes—to see all the people who are here to love and support you and your child. They will come in all shapes and sizes and ages and colors. They may be complete strangers or a member of the special education team. They will become your family—if only for a minute and sometimes for years, and you will be amazed. Let them in. *Let them in.* You will have so much love in your life—it's just not the way you thought it was going to look."

And then I want to say *"Accept. Accept* and *love* this child. Do not mourn for what you think you have lost or are missing out on. Celebrate all that you will experience and receive and be prepared to live in *awe* of it all. Celebrate the joy and wonder of this strange world for which none of us is ever prepared." And then somewhere from the deepest caverns of your mind, you may be reminded that this journey started long before it started. That having had the responsibility for taking care of your aphasic father when you were but eighteen years old is *exactly* the preparation you needed to become Adam's mother. That your wish to have been given even one more day to take your father to the therapies and support him in his recovery absolutely came true. That there is a mysterious synchronicity to it all—you have been the perfect person to have been chosen to be your son's mother. You will be amazed by this insight.

There is nothing more important in my life than having been on this journey. At times it has been awful. At times it has been awesome. I am so grateful to be the mom of Adam—of *All the Adams in the World.*

Acknowledgments

To thank all who have been on this journey with Adam and me for the past 30 years would be an entire book unto itself. However, I would not have been able to write this book without them.

In the early years—I thank the entire therapeutic team at the ICEC, especially Kathy Olivier who was the first to give us hope. To the OCDE Special Education Team of teachers, principals, instructional assistants, specialists and staff, thank you for 19 years of leading us through the best education I could have hoped Adam to receive. Thank you Dr. Marc Lerner, our UCI Infant Specialist, who taught me the importance of treating an entire family and to our Regional Center Advocate, Nikki Strauss, who taught me to get out of my own way. Thanks to Dr. BJ Freeman for teaching us about "the spectrum" and to Dr. Lonnie Lovenger for gifting us the title of our book.

Thank you to Northwest Airlines and Jan Bernal who gave Adam his wings and to Kim DiCuercio for bringing Adam to Camp Kutz.

To Terri Lawson, Pamela Marsden, Mary Holland and Trish Wimbrow-Dwyer, you saved my family throughout the divorce and years thereafter. You listened to me long after I needed to stop crying. Thank you for making sure I stayed on the planet.

Thank you to Susan Elizabeth George, who with great generosity gives us peace of mind.

Thank you to Connie Hall for assuring me that our story needs to be told, even though I doubted that the world needed another book on autism.

To my son, Joshua Wynne, your love and care give me the assurance that I am doing a good job as a mother. And to my son, Adam, thank you for picking me to be your mom. I am grateful to both of my sons every single day.

About the Author

All the Adams in the World is a memoir about the thirty-year life journey shared by a child with severe autism and his mother as together they navigate a world for which they were not prepared—the foreign world of autism. From diagnostic testing as an infant to moving into a group home setting as an adult, each chapter provides an intimate understanding of what Sheila and Adam have experienced while meandering through the many mazes of the medical world, special education, social ostracism, and acceptance. Filled with ups and downs, Sheila tells their story through the many roles she plays as Adam's mother: advocate, conservator, and above all, the person who refuses to give up on her son. Filled with both laughter and tears, Sheila explains how life with Adam is like "*Saturday Night Live* with the Jerry Lewis Telethon running through it." A veteran educator of nearly forty years, Sheila has sat on every side of the IEP table, providing experiences and insights as a parent, general education teacher, special education teacher, and parent mentor. Her hope is that each chapter provides perspectives to parents, siblings, teachers, and medical practitioners who courageously strive to untangle the mysterious world of autism. Her message is one of commitment, hope, and acceptance.

CPSIA information can be obtained
at www.ICGtesting.com
Printed in the USA
JSHW041451050920
7672JS00006B/146